PERCEPTUAL-MOTOR LESSON PLANS
LEVEL-2

BASIC AND "PRACTICAL" LESSON PLANS

FOR PERCEPTUAL-MOTOR PROGRAMS

IN PRESCHOOL AND ELEMENTARY GRADES

by

JACK CAPON

-THIRD EDITION-

1983

EDITOR
Frank Alexander

ARTIST
John Lewis

Published by FRONT ROW EXPERIENCE, 540 Discovery Bay Blvd., Byron, California 94514

15,900 BOOKS IN PRINT AS OF 1994

Copyright Ⓒ FRONT ROW EXPERIENCE 1977

ISBN 0-915256-04-5

Published
by

FRONT ROW EXPERIENCE
540 Discovery Bay Blvd.
Byron, Calif. 94514

CONTENTS

ABOUT THE AUTHOR

Jack Capon is known nationally for his "practical" application of Perceptual-Motor Development to the classroom environment. By means of his numerous workshops conducted every year throughout the United States and Canada, Jack Capon has shown how teachers and others interested in Movement Education can start their own successful program. This book is a further effort by Jack to provide teachers and schools with a practical approach to organizing the physical education program in the elementary grades.

Jack Capon has been in Movement Education since 1956. His present position is with the Alameda City School District of California as Coordinator For Physical Education. The nationally recognized program he developed in Alameda now serves as a model for Perceptual-Motor programs throughout the U.S., Canada, Australia, and New Zealand.

Jack Capon has been very active in Movement Education. Not only in the practical sense of being "out in the field", but through his many other activities. He served 4 years (1968-72) on the Perceptual-Motor Task Force of the American Association for Health, Physical Education and Recreation. He was elected National Chairman of the Elementary Physical Education Section of AAHPER in 1972. Jack served as a consultant for the film "Thinking-Moving-Learning" in 1970, which was his first major effort to promote Perceptual-Motor Development by means of the media. In 1971, he served as co-producer of the record album "Perceptual-Motor Rhythm Games" which combined music with perceptual-motor activities. In 1974, he wrote the first edition of his Level-1 Perceptual-Motor Lesson Plans book plus several other booklets on specific types of equipment activities. His work has been further publicized through numerous articles in various nationally circulated educational magazines.

Jack's Level-2 book presented here provides an easy to implement program with positive results for program participants who have already successfully completed the Level-1 program or who are in the 2nd and 3rd grades. The Level-2 program herein is designed to assist all students, regardless of ability, in refining essential motor skills. The fact that this program (including Level-1) is now being used by teachers and schools throughout the U.S., Canada, Australia, and New Zealand is a testimonial to its "practicality" and effectiveness.

PROGRAM OBJECTIVES

Perceptual-Motor Development refers to one's ability to receive, interpret, and respond successfully to sensory information. "Perception" is the receiving or input system while "motor" refers to output or responsive movement. The environment that the student is placed into will determine the type of sensory stimuli that must be processed. In this Level-2 Perceptual-Motor Program for the 2nd and 3rd grades, participants receive information primarily through the visual, auditory, vestibular, tactile, and kinesthetic senses. All conscious and controlled movement depends on one's ability to interpret sensory information.

Traditionally in physical education programs we have centered our attention on output or performance such as: Can the student jump the rope? Is he or she able to run fast? Does the ball go into the basket? Etc. In Perceptual-Motor Programs we concern ourselves first with input or reception and examine how it affects one's performance. Our awareness of a total process of development now takes on great importance. Program objectives no longer are limited to the acquisition of physical skills and fitness, but rather to assisting the student to function more successfully in all phases of the school curriculum. Our means of accomplishing this goal is through the use of carefully planned movement experiences.

One of the major tasks of the teacher in a Perceptual-Motor Program then becomes that of creating an environment which will demand total mental concentration as well as physical involvement. The student is challenged to think and then respond with purposeful controlled movements. This requires the teacher to develop and maintain a positive working climate.

1

in which students understand fully their responsibilities. It does not mean the program becomes so rigid that the fun and excitement of participating are eliminated, but rather that students are responding with a combination of their best mental and physical efforts.

Perceptual-motor abilities which should be promoted include body image, balance, spatial awareness, hand-eye and foot-eye coordination (visual-motor control), laterality, directionality and proprioception. Attributes of movement such as rhythm, locomotor coordination, agility, strength and flexibility are also developed within various aspects of the program.

PRIMARY OBJECTIVES OF THE LEVEL-2 PROGRAM ARE:
1) Assist each student in acquiring efficient movement.
2) Promote improved sensory functioning.
3) Development of a positive self-image.

The main areas of Program concentration are in promoting improved:
1) Balance Skills (Static and Dynamic)
2) Locomotor Skills (Transport Movements)
3) Manipulation Skills
4) Body and Space Awareness

The need for this type of program in our schools is becoming widely recognized by educational leaders. Students of all ages have a right to move with confidence and control. Schools have an obligation to provide meaningful programs.

AN INTEGRATED PROGRAM

The year's program as presented consists of 25 weekly lesson plans designed for students who have successfully completed the Level-1 Perceptual-Motor Program. Naturally, total application of the Level-2 Program should depend on the specific needs of students and the types of Program activities they have been previously exposed to. The program was successfully field tested at elementary grades 2 and 3 over a 6-year period.

The total program is divided into 3 phases. Phase-1 is organized under the title of Movement Exploration and consists of a weekly problem-solving lesson centered around the use of balls, ropes, hoops, bean bags, rhythm sticks and the parachute. This lesson can easily be conducted indoors (space permitting) or outdoors. Phase-2 involves the traditional game approach and includes one recommended game activity for each 2 weeks of the Program. These game activities would commonly be classified as Low Organized Games. Finally, Phase-3 is the weekly Perceptual-Motor Lessons which consist of 4 different learning stations. The Perceptual-Motor Lessons are designed to be conducted indoors and involve the use of a wide variety of equipment such as the walking board, coordination ladder and jump box.

Activities in all 3 phases of the Level-2 Program (Movement Exploration, Games, and Perceptual-Motor Lessons) have been orgaized into a planned sequence of tasks.

PHASE-1 MOVEMENT EXPLORATION LESSONS
The Movement Exploration activities have been designed to reinforce and compliment the objectives of the Perceptual-Motor Lessons. Each school will need to have basic sets of equipment which the teachers can use to carry out the planned Movement Exploration Lessons. Equipment needed as previously mentioned includes sets of balls, ropes, hoops, bean bags, rhythm sticks and the parachute. A typical class set of Movement Exploration equipment would include, for example, 30 rubber balls stored in a bag or other container. Every student participant in a given lesson should have a piece of equipment to work with. This enables all students to be actively involved in the lesson at all times. Skill is

enhanced due to the fact that many opportunities are provided each participant to practice the challenges and no one is standing in line waiting his or her turn.

In Movement Exploration the teacher or leader presents students with verbal challenges which are in the form of a problem to be solved. Phrases such as "Can you...?", "Who can...?", "Show me how...", "Find a different way...", etc., become the key to motivating students to think and respond with actions which reflect improved skill and movement awareness. Each student is encouraged to solve the problem or challenge in relation to his or her own capabilities. Pre-conceived standards are not set and total involvement reduces the risks of students becoming self-concious and critical of each other. In this non-competitive environment students are normally eager to participate because tasks are presented at a level of comprehension and skill which allows them to experience success. As skill is acquired the difficulty of challenges presented is readily adaptable to the student's interest and ability. Lessons are planned so that skill acquisition becomes a natural outgrowth of participation.

PHASE-2 GAME LESSONS

The Game Lessons are offered as supplemental material to the Level-2 Program. Games normally are not classified as perceptual-motor activities although certainly under the broad umbrella of movement and perceptual experiences they could find a home. Games can help to meet many important needs of elementary grade students and therefore have an important role in the physical education program. Unfortunately, games often become the total physical education program offered in many elementary schools. When this happens, students usually receive a "hit and miss" program with little planning and limited results.

The Games recommended are designed to enrich the total Level-2 Program offered in this book and have been selected with basic needs of students in constant focus. These needs include vigorous activity such as running, the opportunity to develop physical skills such as throwing and catching a ball, learning concepts of sportsmanship and social interaction, leadership opportunities, developing listening skills and the refinement of perceptual-motor abilities such as balance, body and space awareness and directionality.

All Games listed have been used successfully in a pilot program for 6 years. They have been carefully evaluated. Only one game has been suggested for every 2 weeks. This enables teachers to devote more time to carefully teaching an activity and allows the class to enjoy the repetition of playing the game more than once.

The Game sequence has been determined by a number of factors including reinforcement of objectives in the weekly Level-2 Movement Exploration and Perceptual-Motor Lessons, difficulty of skills, complexity of rules and finally their focus as related to goals of the total program. It is strongly recommended that the Games be introduced into the Level-2 Program in the same sequence as presented.

You will enjoy teaching these games and your students will have fun playing them as well as practicing and developing basic skills.

PHASE-3 PERCEPTUAL-MOTOR LESSONS

The perceptual-motor phase of the Level-2 Program is a continuation of the basic station approach used in the Level-1 book. Only one Perceptual-Motor Lesson is offered each week. This lesson is organized so that it may be presented to an entire class as developmental training. However, the teacher may wish to use the results of the recommended Level-2 Perceptual-Motor Evaluation Scale to group students and focus the Perceptual-Motor Lesson on meeting the needs of the motor-deficient student. The Perceptual-Motor Lesson would then become the remedial phase of the Level-2 Program and therefore would be offered only to those students who show a definite need for this type of activity. One of the most difficult assignments facing the teacher is how to meet the needs of the lower ability or poorly coordinated student. The Perceptual-Motor Lesson can serve this purpose in your overall program.

The Level-2 Perceptual-Motor Lessons consist of review activities from the Level-1 Program during the first part of the activites and then gradually introduce more difficult tasks with greater challenges. The philosophy is one of insuring a high degree of success at the start of the program before introducing activities requiring advanced levels of skill. This is especially important if the Program is to be used for remedial training.

PLANNING YOUR PROGRAM

The integrated Perceptual-Motor Lessons are presented to teachers as a guide in setting up a basic Level-2 Perceptual-Motor Program. Teachers will have to decide how much repetition students in their classes need on any given lesson or activity. Teachers also have the responsibility of making modifications in specific activities to insure successful participation for each student in their class.

SEQUENCING OF LESSON ACTIVITIES

One of the most difficult parts of organizing a program of this type is the sequencing of the challenges so that they are appropriate developmentally as well as in terms of skill progression. The Level-2 Program will continue to be evaluated and refined in future editions.

It is important to realize that for each type of lesson in the Program a basic sequence or skill progression has been developed. The main factors in the frequency of inclusion for any one type of activity are the predetermined need for various types of experiences and amount of continuous re-inforcement deemed necessary for the refinement of basic perceptual-motor abilities as found in an average population of elementary school students. It is important to note, however, that teachers should not feel locked into the lesson sequence presented in this Program. It goes without saying that individual needs vary from group to group.

Teachers will find that due to the careful sequencing and organization of the Perceptual-Motor Stations plus the integration of Movement Exploration and Game activities, a high degree of success and interest will be maintained throughout the 25 weeks of the Program.

SETTING UP YOUR CLASSROOM

Each week of the Lesson Plans contains 3 lessons. (First Lesson = Movement Exploration, Second Lesson = Perceptual-Motor Stations and the third Lesson = Games.) Each lesson is designed to last approximately 20 to 30 minutes (20 minutes will often be sufficient for the Movement Exploration and Games Lesson, whereas 30 minutes will normally be required for the Perceptual-Motor Lesson). A typical Perceptual-Motor Lesson has 4 stations. Each station is a separate perceptual-motor activity. The stations are intended to be all run at the same time within your classroom or designated perceptual-motor activity area.

Have your students begin the perceptual-motor activities at the 4 stations programmed for that lesson. Your students should be evenly divided among the stations so that you have approximately the same number of students beginning an activity station at the same time. Students may be grouped either homogenously or heterogenously at each station. It is also best to have each group of students change stations at the same time. This allows for better control and organization. The teacher can determine, in relation to total lesson time available, when the groups should rotate.

In the station examples on the next page:

Students who finish Station 4 go on to Station 1
Students who finish Station 1 go on to Station 2
Students who finish Station 2 go on to Station 3
Students who finish Station 3 go on to Station 4

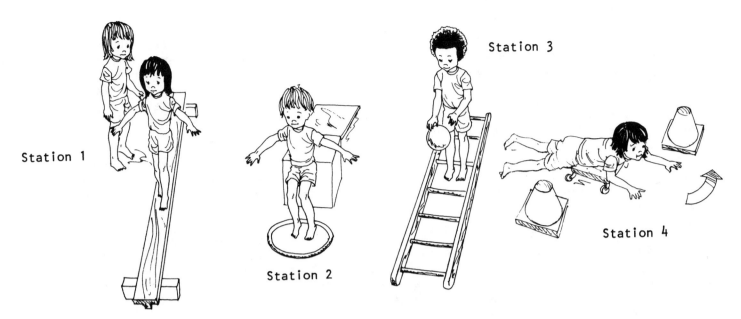

Station 1

Station 2

Station 3

Station 4

Having several activity stations in each lesson allows the students to: proceed faster through all of the activities; receive individualized help; experience a wider variety of perceptual-motor movements; and.....have more "fun".

INTRODUCING THE LESSON

When beginning your Perceptual-Motor Lesson there are 2 common approaches which may be used in orientating your students: 1) Review with the entire class the motor challenges or tasks which the students will engage in at each station. (This can be accomplished quickly by using a student at each station to demonstrate.); or 2) Have an aide at each station explain the activities and present verbal challenges to each group individually as they rotate to that station.

Whether the first or 2nd approach is used depends on the availability of aides at each station plus their insight and ability.

USE OF ADDITIONAL STATIONS

Although only 4 activity or learning stations are included in each lesson, this does not necessarily mean that 4 stations are the ideal number to work with. Certainly if adequate space, equipment and supervision are available, the teacher may desire to use additional stations within each lesson. An important factor to consider here is the number of students involved at each station. Students must be involved in order to have a successful program. An excessive amount of standing in lines and waiting turns defeats the program's purpose. In general, 4 to 6 students at each station is a good guide for class organization. Understandably, due to various limitations, this ratio is not always possible.

In organizing additional learning stations within any given lesson, it is highly recommended that the teacher review activities from previous lessons giving particular attention to those experiences which it is felt are in need of stronger reinforcement. Generally speaking, mat stunts and hand-eye coordination tasks profit most from this opportunity for review.

FACILITY NEEDS

It is of utmost importance to the overall success of the Level-2 Perceptual-Motor Program that an indoor facility be available for storage of equipment and conducting the Program. An empty classroom or multi-purpose room will provide adequate space. (The Movement Exploration and Game Lessons can be accomodated outdoors on the normal playground area.) Upon entering the room to participate, students are asked to remove their shoes and socks. This is done for safety and to provide a better tactile and kinesthetic "feel" for movement as the student interacts with various pieces of equipment.

5

EQUIPMENT

Program equipment plays an important role in helping to develop motor skills. Equipment serves as a catalyst for movement and helps make the program challenging and exciting. However, there is no magic in equipment. The magic is in the student and is brought out in the human interaction between teacher and student. Students need guidance in the correct use of equipment and they need equipment which is appropriate to their size, strength and coordination. The more equipment available, the more involvement of students and hopefully the greater the opportunity for learning.

All of the 20 or so different pieces of equipment used in this program have been carefully selected and designed according to motor development needs of young students There is a definite purpose and reason for every challenge used in conjunction with each piece of equipment.

It should be noted that 3 different levels are incorporated into the Perceptual-Motor Walking Board Challenges. The recommended *low* level is 7" high, the *intermediate* level is 11" high and the *high* level is 20½". For more information on the needs, characteristics and cost of Program equipment, see the sections entitled: Overview Of Basic Perceptual-Motor Equipment, Equipment Construction Diagrams and Perceptual-Motor Equipment Costs.

USE OF AIDES

The use of volunteer aides or upper-grade level students to assist teachers in conducting the program is another vital ingredient to a successful program. The aides can save valuable teaching time by setting up equipment for lessons and then assisting students in acquiring skills at one or more stations. The use of parent aides serves a dual purpose in that the importance of Perceptual-Motor Development can be viewed first hand and community support generated for the Program.

OVERALL PROGRAMMING

The Perceptual-Motor Lesson is the individualized phase of the weekly physical education program. Perceptual-Motor Lessons should be reinforced with large group experiences such as the outlined Movement Exploration and Game activities along with traditional rhythms, relays, apparatus play, etc.

A typical overall weekly plan is presented below as an example of the type of planning necessary for a complete *integrated* physical education program:

Monday	- Movement Exploration Lesson
Tuesday	- Rhythm Activities
Wednesday	- Game Lesson
Thursday	- Review Activity (Games, Exploration, etc.)
Friday	- Perceptual-Motor Lesson

SCREENING

All participants should be screened at the beginning of the Program using the *Level-2 Perceptual-Motor Evaluation Scale* in this book. This Level-2 assessment tool includes testing for a variety of perceptual-motor abilities among which are: balance, body image, spatial awareness, locomotor control and hand-eye coordination. The results of this initial screening should be used to assess individual needs and assist the teacher in grouping students for successful program participation.

PERCEPTUAL-MOTOR TERMINOLOGY

The following terms are used in the Level-2 Lesson Plans and help you accurately assess your students in the *Level-2 Perceptual-Motor Evaluation Scale*.

BODY IMAGE
The individual's concept of his or her body and its' parts. The concept involves the knowledge of: a) the physical structure of the body and its' parts; b) the movements and functions of the body and its' parts; and c) the position of the body and its' parts in relation to each other and to other objects. It forms a base for acquiring an adequate self-concept.

BALANCE
The ability to assume and maintain any body position against the force of gravity. Maintenance of balance results from the interaction of the muscles working to keep the body on its' base.

VISUAL-MOTOR CONTROL
Refers to the ability to successfully integrate visual and motor responses into a physical action. It enables an individual to control movement, and move easily and smoothly from place to place.

COORDINATION
The ability of the body to integrate the action of the muscles of the body to accomplish a specific movement or a series of skilled movements in the most efficient manner.

PROPRIOCEPTION
The awareness of muscular movement and position of the body in space.

GROSS-MOTOR COORDINATION
Results from the development of the skeletal or large muscles to produce efficient total body movement.

FINE-MOTOR COORDINATION
The coordinated use of small muscles resulting from the development of the muscles to the degree that they can perform specific small movements such as cutting, writing, grasping, and so on.

SUSTAINED MOVEMENTS
Motor skills executed consecutively a number of times or continued for an interval of time.

SPACE AWARENESS (SPATIAL ORIENTATION)
Involves the ability to select a reference point to stabilize functions and to organize objects into correct perspective. It involves knowledge of the body and its' position, as well as the positions of other people and objects in relation to one's body in space. Closely associated with body image.

LATERALITY
Internalizing the awareness of: a) the difference between right and left; and b) how far right and how far left various activities are centered. It is the ability to control the two sides of the body together or separately and is the motor basis for spatial concepts. Bilateral movements involve the use of both sides of the body in a simultaneous and parallel fashion as in catching a ball with two hands. Unilateral movements involve the use of one side of the body or one limb on that body side as in bouncing a ball with one hand. Cross-laterality is the simultaneous use of different limbs on opposite sides of the body as in walking where arms and legs move in opposition to each other.

DIRECTIONALITY
Often confused with laterality. An awareness of space outside of the body and involves:
a) knowledge of directions in relation to right and left, in and out, and up and down;
b) the projection of one's self in space; and c) the judging of distances between objects.

HAND-EYE COORDINATION
Refers to one's ability to use his or her eyes and hands together to accomplish a task.

FOOT-EYE COORDINATION
Refers to one's ability to use his or her eyes and feet together to accomplish a task.

OCULAR PURSUIT
Ability of the eyes to work together in following (tracking) a moving object or in focusing from one object to another.

KINESTHESIS
One's awareness of muscular movement and expenditure of energy during the performance of a skill.

PERCEPTUAL-MOTOR SKILLS
Those skills which indicate the interrelationships between the perceptual or sensory processes and motor activity and the ability of the individual to receive, interpret, and respond accurately to stimuli, either internal or external. Perceptual-motor learning involves all senses: seeing, hearing, touching, tasting, smelling, and moving or kinesthesis. Also known as "Sensory-Motor Skills".

BEFORE YOU START

Don't forget to screen your students by using the *Level-2 Perceptual-Motor Evaluation Scale* or a similar assessment instrument. Also, by testing your students again half-way through your program and at the end, you will be able to note the progress of your students and to help them be successful in those areas where they need improvement.

Before beginning your 25 week integrated Perceptual-Motor Program, go over the following Checklist. The Checklist contains important reminders of things to do, to be aware of, and to watch for *before you start*.

CHECKLIST

1) Assist students with clothing problems. All participants are asked to remove shoes and socks before going to the Perceptual-Motor Stations.

2) Explain lesson tasks to participants at assigned station.

3) Instruct students in correct technique and skill needed for successful participation.

4) Use student to "model" or demonstrate task, if necessary, for correct performance.

5) Provide physical assistance (hold hands, etc.), if needed, for emotional security and confidence, but gradually remove this "crutch".

6) Reinforce positive behavior of students by providing verbal recognition of successful performance.

7) Modify tasks where applicable for successful performance.

8) Add extra equipment whenever possible (in relation to available space) to allow greater involvement. Example: use several rebound nets or launching boards, if available, not just one.

9) If both walking boards (that is, low and intermediate/high) are involved in a lesson, have students perform on each board and rotate back and forth.

10) Sometimes it is best to group students by motor deficiencies or strengths so that tasks can be more easily modified or adapted to individual abilities and needs.

11) At some stations students will receive many repetitions during a given lesson while at another station the repetitions will be limited. This cannot be helped due to the many different types of equipment and tasks or challenges used in the program.

12) The number of repetitions is not the key factor in learning---the quality of each trial is more important.

13) It is best to have students work at one station for a period of time (7 to 10 minutes) and then all groups rotate at the same time (on signal from the teacher) to a new station.

14) Success is the greatest motivator of all! Be aware of each student's ability level and make necessary task adjustments (that is, lower cross bar or jump standard, place tires closer, etc.) to insure a high degree of success.

15) Whenever time allows after students have received several repetitions in "directed or structured" tasks, challenge them to discover or find a new way of performing. This allows each student to use his own creativity and skill.

16) Remember---this is a learning program. If students are not mentally involved in terms of thinking and planning their motor responses to a given task or challenge, then results will be limited in terms of stated objectives.

SAFETY FIRST

Safety should be constantly stressed so that both students and aides are aware of their responsibilities in this important area. Participation should not be allowed without adult supervision.

Equipment must be checked on a regular basis to insure that it is safe for use. Wood equipment especially needs to be maintained free of splinters, cracks, etc. Some equipment items such as jump boxes, incline boards, and scooter boards may be carpeted for extra safety.

Improper clothing is probably the greatest safety hazard in any perceptual-motor program. Long dresses and slippery leotards worn by girls are among the biggest clothing problems. Some types of shoes and boots can be very awkward and slippery to move in. Students are safest in their bare feet.

Before the start of your program, you should advise parents of the need for their children to wear specific types of clothing on days when your Perceptual-Motor Program is conducted. If you schedule the same days each week for your motor activities, then parental cooperation will be easier to accomplish.

Other safety factors to be taken into consideration are as follows:
  1) Allow only one person on the equipment at a time.
  2) Insist that students get into a good starting position before beginning any task.
  3) Be sure to allow enough space for safe movements.
  4) Stress control of movements at all times rather than speed.
  5) Insist on strong mental concentration when responding to each challenge. "Showing off" can lead to serious accidents!

PERCEPTUAL-MOTOR EVALUATION SCALE
LEVEL-2

Before beginning any comprehensive program in motor development, participants should be assessed as to their strengths and weaknesses. Obviously there are countless numbers of screening tasks and surveys which are available for use as an assessment instrument. This *Level-2 Perceptual-Motor Evaluation Scale* is provided for teachers because it is easy to administer, takes only a limited amount of instruction time and provides information (as recorded on the *Record Sheet*) which teachers can easily use to plan purposeful program activities. It also provides teachers with a tool which may be used to evaluate student progress and program effectiveness.

GENERAL INSTRUCTIONS

1) Tests are designed so that they may be administered as a part of the physical education class period.

2) Do not tell the students they are being "tested". Make the screening a natural part of your physical education period.

3) Students are given an "S" for *Satisfactory Performance* and an "N" for *Needs Improvement*.

4) Students receiving an "N" should be retested in the middle and/or at the end of your Perceptual-Motor Program.

5) Demonstration of test items to show correct response is permissible. You are observing performance, not testing ability to interpret verbal directions.

6) If judgement of a student's performance is uncertain, you may wish to have him or her repeat the activity.

7) Test items may be administered over a period of a few weeks, or over a period of a few days at the teacher's discretion.

8) Remember, the main purpose of the screening program is to "look" at each student as an individual and as a result, plan Program activities which will take into account individual needs.

TASK <1> WALKING BOARD

PERFORMANCE OBJECTIVES
By walking forward and backward on a walking board with eyes focused on teacher's hand at eye level, student demonstrates balance, laterality and visual-motor control.

EQUIPMENT
Walking board and mats.

PROCEDURE
Teacher stands at opposite end of board from student. Ask student to walk the board *forward* with eyes focusing on teacher's hand held at eye level of student. Upon reaching end of board, student walks *backwards* on board until reaching starting position. Eyes still remain focused on teacher's hand while walking backwards on board.

EVALUATION
If student shows any difficulty such as stepping off board, sliding feet, pausing frequently, or uses a fast walk to avoid losing balance, mark an "N" for *Needs Improvement*.

TASK ⟨2⟩ CRISS-CROSS WALK

PERFORMANCE OBJECTIVES

By using a cross-over step up and down the length of a rope, student demonstrates laterality, foot-eye coordination and dynamic balance.

EQUIPMENT

Long rope and 2 bike tires.

PROCEDURE

Use one extended long jump rope (approximately 14 feet) or 2 short jump ropes (approximately 7 feet each) tied together. Student is asked to walk *forward* to end of rope using a cross-over (*scissors*) step and then return to starting position by walking *backwards* using a cross-over step. Student should be asked not to watch feet. Teacher may wish to use hand as a fixation point.

EVALUATION

If student is unable to smoothly coordinate steps (loses balance, moves wrong foot, steps on rope repeatedly, etc.), pauses frequently, or continuously watches feet, mark an "N" for *Needs Improvement*.

TASK ⟨3⟩ HOPPING

PERFORMANCE OBJECTIVES

By pausing and hopping on first the right foot, then the left foot, through the 4 tires, student demonstrates gross-motor coordination, static and dynamic balance, foot-eye coordination and space awareness.

EQUIPMENT

Four bike tires.

PROCEDURE

Use four 18" bike tires placed end to end. Student is asked to support weight on *right* foot inside the first bike tire and hold it for 6 seconds (slow count of 6). Student then hops forward away from teacher 3 hops in succession on this same foot, landing in a tire on each hop. Student then turns facing the teacher and supports weight on *left* foot and holds it for 6 seconds inside the 4th tire. This is followed by 3 hops in succession on this same foot, each hop landing in a tire.

EVALUATION

If opposite foot touches ground while either stationary or hopping, or postural shift is not smooth, lacks rhythm, loses control, etc., or foot hits tire or fails to land within confines of tire, mark an "N" for *Needs Improvement*.

TASK ⟨4⟩ AGILITY SKIP

PERFORMANCE OBJECTIVES

By skipping around obstacles in a figure-eight pattern, student demonstrates gross-motor coordination, agility, rhythm and directionality.

EQUIPMENT

Three traffic cones.

PROCEDURE

From a starting line, place 3 traffic cones spaced at 5 foot intervals as shown. Student is instructed to *skip* around and between cones in a figure-eight pattern and end up back at the starting line.

EVALUATION

If student is unable to alternate feet in a smooth rhythmic skip, or becomes confused in direction of movement, mark an "N" for *Needs Improvement*.

TASK <5> BALL DRIBBLING

PERFORMANCE OBJECTIVES
By dribbling a ball around 2 obstacles, student demonstrates hand-eye coordination.

EQUIPMENT
Ball and 2 traffic cones.

PROCEDURE
Place 2 traffic cones approximately 10 to 12 feet apart.
Student starts next to one cone and dribbles a 7"
rubber ball (using one hand only) down and around
opposite cone and back to the first cone.

EVALUATION
If student loses control of ball, uses 2 hands on dribble at
same time, or stops dribble, mark an "N" for *Needs Improvement*.

TASK <6> ROPE JUMPING

PERFORMANCE OBJECTIVES
By jumping a jump rope in succession, student demonstrates
gross-motor coordination, rhythm and visual-motor control.

EQUIPMENT
Jump rope.

PROCEDURE
Student begins with short jump rope (approximately 7' long) held in
hands and resting in back of heels. On signal to begin, student attempts to jump the rope 5 times in succession without a miss. Rope
must be turned over head on each jump and student must jump the
rope with both feet at once, *not skip the rope*. (Teacher may wish
to give student second opportunity on this test, if it is felt
that student was not given fair opportunity to perform.)

EVALUATION
If student is unable to jump the rope 5 times in succession without a miss or lacks rhythm, mark an "N" for *Needs Improvement*.

TASK <7> OPTIONAL TESTS

The teacher may wish to run an additional screening check on students, for example, a
screening test designed to add additional information for assessing individual needs in
hand-eye and fine-motor coordination.

RECORD TEST RESULTS ON *RECORD SHEET* ON THE FOLLOWING PAGE

LEVEL-2

PERCEPTUAL-MOTOR EVALUATION SCALE

— RECORD SHEET —

MARKING N = Needs Improvement S = Satisfactory	Task 1 Walking Board		Task 2 Criss-Cross Walk		Task 3 Hopping		Task 4 Agility Skip		Task 5 Ball Dribbling		Task 6 Rope Jumping		Task 7 Optional	
NAME	Fall	Spr.	Fall	Spr.	Fall	Spr.	Fall	Spr.	Fall	Spr.	Fall	Spr.	Fall	Spr.
1														
2														
3														
4														
5														
6														
7														
8														
9														
10														
11														
12														
13														
14														
15														
16														
17														
18														
19														
20														
21														
22														
23														
24														
25														
26														
27														
28														
29														
30														

copy this page to make your own record sheet

PERFORMANCE OBJECTIVES
   By performing the following challenges, student demonstrates ability
   in bouncing and catching ball, and in tossing and catching ball.

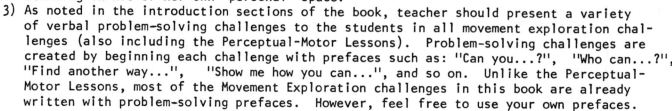

(1)

EQUIPMENT
   Classroom set of rubber balls.

TEACHING SUGGESTIONS
   1) All participants should have a ball in
      their possession to begin the lesson.
   2) A "scatter" formation is used with each student
      standing in his or her own "personal" space.
   3) As noted in the introduction sections of the book, teacher should present a variety
      of verbal problem-solving challenges to the students in all movement exploration chal-
      lenges (also including the Perceptual-Motor Lessons). Problem-solving challenges are
      created by beginning each challenge with prefaces such as: "Can you...?", "Who can...?",
      "Find another way...", "Show me how you can...", and so on. Unlike the Perceptual-
      Motor Lessons, most of the Movement Exploration challenges in this book are already
      written with problem-solving prefaces. However, feel free to use your own prefaces.

CHALLENGES
   1) Can you bounce and catch the ball with 2 hands?
   2) Who can bounce and catch the ball 10 times in a row without dropping it?
   3) Now see if you can bounce the ball, clap your hands and catch the ball.
   4) Try tossing the ball above your head, let it bounce and then catch it.
   5) Show me how you can toss the ball above your
      head, let it bounce, turn around and catch it.
   6) Who can bounce the ball under each leg and catch it?
   7) This time try to toss the ball above your head and catch it without moving your feet.
   8) Can you toss the ball above your head, clap your hands, and then catch the ball?
   9) How many times can you clap your hands before catching the ball?
  10) Show me how you can toss the ball into the air, jump off the ground and catch it.
  11) Who can toss the ball from hand to hand like a juggler?
  12) How would you hold the ball using just your elbows?
  13) Now hold the ball between your knees. Can you jump like
      a kangaroo by keeping the ball between your knees?
  14) Can you jump in a circle and still keep the ball between you knees?
  15) Show me how you would hold the ball between your feet,
      jump off the ground and catch the ball in the air.
  16) Who can hold the ball in back of their head, re-
      lease it, and then catch it behind their back?
  17) Place your ball on the ground and see if you can jump
      forward over the ball and then backward over the ball.
  18) How many other ways can you move over your ball?

Lesson 2   STATION ◁1▷ LOW AND INTERMEDIATE WALKING BOARDS   1st Week

PERFORMANCE OBJECTIVES
   By walking over an obstacle on the low board and walking forward
   with eyes focused on teacher's hand on intermediate board, student
   demonstrates visual-motor control, dynamic balance and laterality.

(1)

EQUIPMENT
   Low and intermediate walking board and cross bar with mats.

CHALLENGES
   1) *LOW BOARD* - Walk forward, step over cross bar

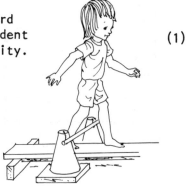

placed across the center of the walking board.
2) *INTERMEDIATE BOARD* - Walk forward with eyes focusing on teacher's hand.

STRESS: *INTERMEDIATE BOARD* - Walk slowly, head erect, eyes
on hand, using arms to adjust body weight.

Lesson 2   STATION ◁2▷ MAT STUNTS   1st Week

PERFORMANCE OBJECTIVES
   By *alligator crawling* and creeping, student demonstrates loco-   (1)
   motor coordination, cross-laterality, and kinesthetic awareness.

EQUIPMENT
   Mats.
                                                                           (2)
CHALLENGES
   1) Crawl on stomach using bent arms and legs to maneuver
      body. This is called an *alligator crawl*.
   2) Creep forward on hands and knees.

STRESS: Cross-pattern movements using opposite arm and leg in coordination.
        Speed is *not* important. Students move down mats in one direction only!

Lesson 2   STATION ◁3▷ BEAN BAG TOSS INTO TIRES   1st Week

PERFORMANCE OBJECTIVES
   By tossing bean bag into tires with alternate
   hands, student demonstrates hand-eye coordination, laterality, and directionality.   (1)

EQUIPMENT
   Classroom set of bean bags and 6 bike tires.

CHALLENGES
   1) From behind a restraining line, student is
      given 3 underhand tosses on each turn and
      attempts to get one bean bag into each tire.
      (Student must get one bean bag into first tire before trying for 2nd tire,
      etc. Use at least 2 tossing areas. Painted bike tires serve as targets.)
   2) Students successful with preferred hand may try opposite hand, or distance may be increased.

STRESS: Stepping forward with opposite foot from throwing hand to transfer weight into toss
        (cross-lateral movement), and following through toward target with tossing hand.

Lesson 2   STATION ◁4▷ JUMP BOX   1st Week

PERFORMANCE OBJECTIVES
   By jumping from jump box onto mat or into tire target, student demonstrates dynamic balance, locomotor control, and space awareness.   (3)

EQUIPMENT
   Jump box with incline board, red bike tire and mats.

CHALLENGES
   1) Walk up incline board onto jump box,
      take correct jumping position, release
      with both feet at once and land on *mat*.
   2) Run up incline board and
      jump from box onto mat.
   3) Same as in (1) and (2) only add red

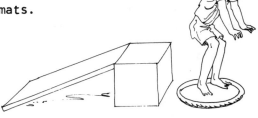

15

bike tire which student must land inside of with good balance and control.

STRESS: Controlled landing (catch weight and freeze) with knees bent. Student lands "softly"
on front part of feet to cushion body. Arms are lowered to "break" movement as feet
contact mat.

Lesson 3   GAME - *5-Around*   1st & 2nd Week

PERFORMANCE OBJECTIVES
By performing in the *5-Around*
game, student demonstrates
ball handling (passing and
catching) skills.

EQUIPMENT
Two balls.

DIRECTIONS
1) Divide class in half
with each group or
team forming a circle.
2) The 2 circles will compete
against each other, using
whatever type of ball the teacher
wishes to use (preferably 2 rubber balls).
3) One student in each circle will hold the ball for his circle over his head, and upon
a signal to start, will pass the ball to the person on his right. When the ball has
traveled around the circle once to the student who started passing it, everyone in
that circle will yell: "ONE"!
4) Each circle will continue to pass the ball around in the same direction, and each
time it reaches the head student the group will yell out the repetition, for example,
"TWO"!, then "THREE"!, and so on until the number called out has reached "5-Around".
5) The first circle to successfully complete the number of cycles will be the winner.
(Teacher may change game for variation to "10-Around".)
6) Each student must handle the ball each time it travels around the circle, or the
circle is disqualified.
7) They must pass the ball, not hand it around!
8) Teacher may elect to give the first team reaching "5-Around" one point.
9) First team scoring a pre-selected number of points (example... 3 points) would be
declared the overall class winner.

TEACHING SUGGESTIONS
1) Teach students to carefully watch the ball and have
their hands ready (form pocket) to catch the ball.
2) Have students use a two-handed underhand pass for good control of the ball.
3) Equal spacing of students around the circle is important for team success.

Lesson 1   MOVEMENT EXPLORATION WITH ROPES   2nd Week

PERFORMANCE OBJECTIVES
By performing the following challenges, student
demonstrates ability to perform walking patterns
with rope on ground, jumping patterns with rope
on ground, and hopping patterns with rope on ground.

EQUIPMENT
Classroom set of jump ropes.

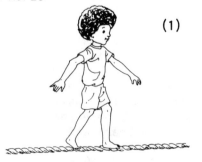
(1)

TEACHING SUGGESTIONS
1) All participants should have a rope in their possession.
2) Ropes are placed on the ground and student stands at far end of rope ready to respond to verbal challenges presented by the teacher.

CHALLENGES
1) Can you walk on the rope down to the end and back without turning around?
2) Walking very tall, who can walk the length of the rope touching their heel against their toe with each step?
3) Who can, while touching their heel to their toe with each step, walk backwards the length of the rope?
4) Can you walk to the end of your rope and back by moving sideways? (Walk on the rope.)
5) Show me how you would walk forward to the end of your rope and back using a scissors (*criss-cross*) walk. Avoid touching the rope.
6) Now, can you walk backwards down and back using a *scissors walk*?
7) How would you jump with 2 feet around your rope without touching it?
8) Keeping the rope between your legs, who can jump down to the end and back without turning around?
9) Can you jump down to the end and back, but each time you jump, land on the opposite side of your rope?
10) Find another way of jumping down to the end of your rope and back. (For example: sideways, jump and turn, etc.)
11) Who can hop on their right foot all around their rope without touching it?
12) Now hop on your left foot around your rope without touching it.
13) Show me how you can hop down to the end of your rope and back, but each time you hop, land on the opposite side of your rope.
14) Who can hop down to the end of their rope using one foot and back on the other foot without losing their balance?
15) Find a different way of moving down to the end of your rope and back without touching the rope, but you must keep the rope between your legs at all times.

Lesson 2   STATION ◁1▷ LOW AND INTERMEDIATE WALKING BOARDS   2nd Week

PERFORMANCE OBJECTIVES
By balancing bean bag on head on low board and stepping into and over obstacles on intermediate board, student demonstrates dynamic balance, laterality, and visual-motor coordination.

(2)

EQUIPMENT
Low walking board with bean bag, and intermediate walking board with cross bar, 2 bike tires and mats.

CHALLENGES
1) *LOW BOARD* - Walk forward to center of board, pick up bean bag, place on head, walk to end of board.
2) *INTERMEDIATE BOARD* - Walk forward, step into tires, and over cross bar.

STRESS: *LOW BOARD* - Student should bend knees and lower body down to pick up bean bag, not stooping from waist. Eyes focus on bean bag, not down at feet. *INTERMEDIATE BOARD* - The eyes shift from one visual target to another, but do not watch feet. Movements are performed slowly!

Lesson 2   STATION ◁2▷ OBSTACLE COURSE   2nd Week

PERFORMANCE OBJECTIVES
By going over, under, and through obstacles, student demonstrates body and space awareness, directionality, and locomotor control.

17

EQUIPMENT
Mats, 2 cross bars, and car tire with holder.

(2)

CHALLENGES
1) Jump over cross bar from a *stationary* position. (Adjust height of bar to ability level of participants.)
2) Crawl under low cross bar. (Student in prone position.)
3) Crawl through auto tire supported in tire holder.
4) After student has experienced success with the above challenges (2 or 3 repetitions), challenge student to find a different way of moving through the obstacles.

STRESS: Student attempts to go over, under, and through without touching any of the obstacles with his body.

Lesson 2   STATION ◁3▷ COORDINATION LADDER   2nd Week

(1)

PERFORMANCE OBJECTIVES
By moving across the coordination ladder, student demonstrates foot-eye coordination, dynamic balance, and space awareness.

EQUIPMENT
Coordination ladder and mats.

CHALLENGES
1) *Balance walk* forward on rungs of ladder.
2) Run between the rungs of the ladder.
3) Challenge student to create own pattern of movement. ("Show me a different way...", etc.)

STRESS: Eyes must guide movement! One student moves at a time on the ladder. Allow repetition of tasks. Student moves only as fast as complete body control can be maintained.

Lesson 2   STATION ◁4▷ BALL BOUNCING WITH TIRES   2nd Week

(1)

PERFORMANCE OBJECTIVES
By bouncing and catching the ball while jumping and hopping across the tire pattern, student demonstrates hand-eye coordination, space awareness, and locomotor coordination.

EQUIPMENT
Ball and 5 bike tires.

CHALLENGES
1) Student bounces and catches ball once in each of 5 tires followed by a jump into each of the tires.
2) Student hops through tires on one foot and bounces ball into each tire. (Bouncing of ball into tire precedes the hop.)
3) After student is successful on a few trials with challenges (1) and (2), challenge student to find a different way of moving through the tires with the ball.

STRESS: Student bounces ball into tire followed by a jump into same tire. Both feet leave ground at same time on each jump. Eyes focus on ball with hands and fingers forming a pocket to properly catch ball.

PERFORMANCE OBJECTIVES
   By performing the following challenges, student demonstrates
   balancing skills, jumping skills, and hopping skills.

EQUIPMENT
   Classroom set of hoops.

(1)

TEACHING SUGGESTIONS
   1) All participants should have a hoop in their possession.
   2) Hoops are placed on ground, and student stands in center of hoop
      ready to respond to verbal challenges presented by the teacher.
   3) Hoops must be spaced far enough apart so that students
      do not interfere with each other as they begin moving.

CHALLENGES
   1) Can you balance on one foot in the center of your hoop?
   2) How low can you go keeping your weight on this same foot?
   3) Show me how tall you can make yourself while balancing on your other foot.
   4) Who can balance on one foot and one hand? Can you add the
      other hand so that you are balancing on 3 body parts?
   5) Find a way of balancing inside your hoop by using 5 body parts.
   6) How would you balance your body with 2 body parts touching inside
      your hoop and 2 parts touching outside your hoop?
   7) Who can jump up and down 10 times in the center of their hoop?
   8) This time, try jumping 5 times in the center of your hoop, but
      each jump must be a little higher than the one before.
   9) Can you jump forward out of your hoop and then jump backwards into your hoop?
   10) Now try jumping backwards out of your hoop, then jump forward into
       your hoop. (Next have students combine jumping challenges 9 and 10.)
   11) Find another way of jumping out of your hoop and then back into
       your hoop. (For example: sideways, jump and turn, etc.)
   12) Show me how far outside your hoop you can jump, but you must land with complete con-
       trol over your body, and freeze (stop) when you land. This is called a *long jump*.
   13) Your new challenge is to try and jump back into your hoop with one big jump.
   14) Who can jump around their hoop keeping one foot on the inside and one foot on
       the outside of the hoop. Without changing your feet, can you jump backwards?
   15) How would you jump around your hoop with each jump landing on a different side of
       your hoop? (For example: inside, outside, etc.)
   16) Can you hop 5 times on your left foot, then 5 times on your right foot inside your hoop?
   17) Who can hop around the outside of their hoop on one foot?
   18) This time, I would like to see you hop around your hoop on one foot, but when
       I blow the whistle (or clap hands) you must change feet and change directions.
   19) Can you hop around your hoop on one foot and land on different
       sides of your hoop with each hop? (Inside, outside, etc.)
   20) Find a different way of moving around your hoop.

PERFORMANCE OBJECTIVES
   By kneeling on one knee on the low board and stepping
   over the coiled rope on the intermediate board, student demonstrates dynamic balance, laterality and
   visual-motor coordination.

(2)

EQUIPMENT
   Low and intermediate walking boards, rope and mats.

CHALLENGES
1) *LOW BOARD* - Walk forward to middle of board, kneel on one knee, rise and walk to end.
2) *INTERMEDIATE BOARD* - Walk forward using "snake" rope as visual target. (Student attempts to step into spaces provided by rope which is coiled around the board.)

STRESS: *LOW BOARD* - Student kneels on each side of body (alternates knees). *INTERMEDIATE BOARD* - Student places feet in spaces provided by rope and is careful not to step on the sleeping "snake" (rope).

Lesson 2   STATION ◆2◆ MAT STUNTS   3rd Week

PERFORMANCE OBJECTIVES
By performing a *dog run* and *lame dog run*, student demonstrates laterality, locomotor coordination, and upper arm and shoulder strength.

(1)

EQUIPMENT
Mats.

CHALLENGES
1) *Dog run* with weight distributed evenly on hands and feet (4-legged run).
2) *Lame dog run* on 2 hands and one leg (3-legged run with weight on hands and hopping with one leg forward).

(2)

STRESS: *DOG RUN* - Weight forward on hands. Move only as fast as complete body control and coordination can be maintained. *LAME DOG RUN* - Hands may move at same time or may alternate.

Lesson 2   STATION ◆3◆ JUMP BOX   3rd Week

PERFORMANCE OBJECTIVES
By running and walking up to jump box and jumping into tire of choice, student demonstrates dynamic balance, kinesthetic awareness, space awareness, and directionality.

(1)

EQUIPMENT
Jump box with incline board, 3 bike tires and mats.

CHALLENGES
1) Walk up incline board onto jump box, take good jumping position with feet spread, release both feet at once, and jump into tire of choice (3 tires are used).
2) Run up incline board and perform same task as in (1) above.

STRESS: Bending of knees on take-off and landing. Student lands with complete body control (freeze) in tire of choice. Student cushions body by landing "softly" on front part of feet (not flat-footed).

Lesson 2   STATION ◆4◆ BEAN BAG TOSS AND LAUNCHING BOARD   3rd Week

PERFORMANCE OBJECTIVES
By catching bean bag from rebound net, and by launching and catching bean bags from a launching board, student demonstrates hand-eye coordination and foot-eye coordination.

EQUIPMENT
  Rebound net, launching board and classroom set of bean bags.

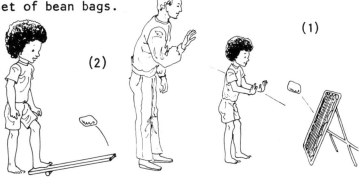

CHALLENGES
  1) *REBOUND NET - Reaction catching* with
     teacher or aide throwing bags against
     net and student catching. Teacher
     throws fast or slow depending on stu-
     dent's ability to react, track, and
     catch bean bag. Each student is given
     5 chances to catch bean bag and drops
     bag as soon as it is caught so that
     he or she is ready to catch the next one.
  2) *LAUNCHING BOARD* - Student steps on end of board, launches, eye tracks, and catches
     bean bag. Student has 5 trials on each turn and attempts to catch 5 bags in a row.

STRESS: Eyes watch bean bag into hands. Hands move as a unit to the target
          (bean bag) and form a pocket to catch the bean bag. In Challenge (2)
          student strikes board with heel of foot for necessary force.

Lesson 3   GAME - *SHIPWRECK*   3rd & 4th Week

PERFORMANCE OBJECTIVES
  By performing in the *Shipwreck* game,
  student demonstrates listening skills,
  space awareness, and agility movements.

○○○○○○○○○○○○○○

Line Up In The Galley

EQUIPMENT
  None.

DIRECTIONS
  1) All students are designated as members of the "Ship's Crew" and take a scatter position
     within the designated playing area. Playing area may be a multi-purpose room, turf
     area, basketball court, etc. They imagine they are on the deck of a ship.
  2) Various verbal challenges (commands) are given by the teacher or leader so
     that students must think and react quickly.
       a) "Line up in the galley!" Students quickly form a straight
          line down the center of the playing area.
       b) "Man the lifeboats!" Students run to left side wall, or left side boundary line.
       c) "Man the quarterdeck!" Students run to right side wall or right side boundary line.
       d) "Hit the deck!" Students quickly lay down on the floor or ground. Depending on
          type of playing surface, teachers may wish to modify response to *squatting down low.*
       e) "Man overboard!" Students assume a position on their backs with feet and hands in
          the air. This command may also be modified, if necessary, to students taking a
          crab walk position (weight on hands and feet with stomach facing up).
       f) "Freeze!" Students stop in place and hold position with no movement. This
          command can be given any time players are moving in one direction or another.

TEACHING SUGGESTIONS
  1) Stress to players that they must think before they move.
  2) Challenges can be given in any sequence desired. Occasionally the same
     challenge may be repeated twice in succession to keep players alert.

Lesson 1   MOVEMENT EXPLORATION WITH PARACHUTE   4th Week

PERFORMANCE OBJECTIVES
  By performing the following challenges, student demonstrates
  group teamwork (listening skills), and inflating parachute.

EQUIPMENT
Classroom-size parachute and 3 balls.

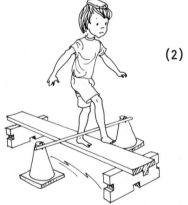

TEACHING SUGGESTIONS
1) Students should be evenly spaced around the parachute using an *overhand* grip (palms down).
2) Have students roll the edge of chute about 5 rolls (depends on design and size of chute) toward the center for a firmer grip.
3) Adapt problem solving prefaces such as "Can you...?", "Show me how you can...", etc., to the challenges.

CHALLENGES
1) *OCEAN WAVES* - shake the chute up and down.
2) *INFLATION (UMBRELLA)* - inflate the parachute up over your heads.
3) *TENTING* - inflate the parachute up over your heads and walk 3 steps in towards the center to cause the parachute to billow up like a large tent.
4) *HIDE-A-WAY (IGLOO)* - inflate the parachute as in tenting, and then seal yourselves inside of the chute (canopy).
5) *FLY AWAY* - inflate the parachute, and on signal, all release the parachute at the same time.
6) *WILD HORSE PULL* - grip the parachute with your backs toward the chute. On signal, all begin pulling like a tug-a-war contest.
7) *WRIST ROLL* - hold the parachute at your waist level, and on a signal, begin rolling it towards the center keeping your arms straight and the canopy pulled tight.
8) *BEND AND STRETCH* - bend down and touch the chute to your toes and then stretch as high as possible. (This sequence is repeated on a count.)
9) *POPCORN* - (Three balls are placed on the canopy.) shake the parachute up and down to pop the balls up in the air, but do not let them come off the canopy.
10) *BALL SHAKE* - (Class is divided into 2 or 3 teams.) Shake the balls up and down, but do not let them come off on your team's side of the parachute.

Lesson 2   STATION ◁1▷ LOW AND INTERMEDIATE WALKING BOARDS   4th Week

PERFORMANCE OBJECTIVES
By walking and turning at center of low board, and by picking up and balancing bean bag on head while going over obstacle on intermediate board, student demonstrates balance, tactile awareness, and visual-motor coordination.

(2)

EQUIPMENT
Low and intermediate walking boards, cross bar, bean bag, and mats.

CHALLENGES
1) *LOW BOARD* - Walk forward to center of board, make a half-turn, and walk backward to end of board.
2) *INTERMEDIATE BOARD* - Walk forward, pick up bean bag, place on head, walk forward and step over cross bar, and walk to end of board.

STRESS: *INTERMEDIATE BOARD* - Student should bend knees and lower body down to pick up bean bag, not stooping from waist. Eyes focus on targets (bean bag, then cross bar), not looking down at feet.

22

PERFORMANCE OBJECTIVES
By jumping forward, sideways, and twisting body in mid-air for alignment in the tire pattern, student demonstrates locomotor coordination, balance, space awareness, directionality, and motor planning ability.

EQUIPMENT
Six bike tires, and 5 ropes.

CHALLENGES
1) First have student jump forward and side-ways through the pattern as indicated in the illustration. (Sideways jump from tires 1 to 2, 3 to 4, & 5 to 6.)
2) Next have student jump through the pattern in the same direction as before, but body position must be changed (twist body) during each jump so that landing is made facing in the direction of next jump as shown by the arrows. For example: student shown in illustration is facing the wrong way for the next jump into the 6th tire. Therefore, student must twist body in mid-air so as to land facing the last tire in the movement pattern as shown by the arrows.

STRESS: Bending of knees on take off and landing of each jump. Both feet leave floor at the same time on each jump.

PERFORMANCE OBJECTIVES
By moving along a coordination ladder, student demonstrates loco-motor skill and coordination, balance, and space awareness.

EQUIPMENT
Coordination ladder and mats.

CHALLENGES
1) Jump between rungs of ladder placed on mats or rug.
2) Jump into every other (or alternate) space between the rungs.
3) Four legged walk between or on rungs of ladder.
4) *Balance walk* forward on side rails of ladder (one foot on each side).

STRESS: Both feet leave ground at same time on jump. Student carefully guides feet so that they do not trip on rungs of ladder.

PERFORMANCE OBJECTIVES
By dribbling a ball around a cone pattern, student demonstrates hand-eye coordination, visual memory ability, and directionality.

EQUIPMENT
Three traffic cones and a ball.

CHALLENGES
1) Dribble ball (using one hand) around obstacles in pattern as shown. If unable to control ball with one-handed dribble, student may try dribbling with both hands. (Students not ready for this task may use a modified bounce and catch.)

STRESS: Student attempts to follow the directed pattern. Finger
        tips control the ball by using a push and not a slap.

Lesson 1   MOVEMENT EXPLORATION WITH BEAN BAGS   5th Week

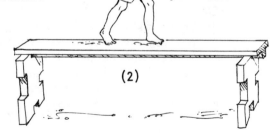

(5)

PERFORMANCE OBJECTIVES
 By performing the following challenges, student demonstrates throwing and catching skills.

EQUIPMENT
 Classroom set of bean bags.

TEACHING SUGGESTIONS
 1) All participants should have a bean bag
   in their possession to begin the lesson.
 2) Students are in a scatter formation on the playground. There should be enough space
   allowed between participants so that they do not interfere with each other's performance.

CHALLENGES
 1) Can you throw (under-hand toss) your bean bag upward and
   catch it by using both hands *without* moving your feet?
 2) Can you throw your bean bag upward and catch it with one hand without moving your feet?
 3) Show me how you can catch it above your head. (Emphasize correct
   finger position--pointed upward and slightly back towards head.)
 4) Now show me how you can catch it below your head level. (Review correct
   position of fingers--pointed forward with palms up, forming a pocket.)
 5) Who can toss their bean bag upward with one hand and catch it by using the other hand?
 6) Can you change back and forth from tossing to catching by using opposite hands?
 7) Show me how you can throw the bean bag up above your head, and
   then jump up and catch it at the highest possible point.
 8) Now try throwing the bean bag up above your head, clap your hands, and catch it.
 9) Can you clap 2 times and catch it?
 10) How many times can you clap your hands before catching the bean bag?
 11) Placing the bean bag on 2 hands with your palms up, can **you** flip it ½
    turn and catch it? (*Flip the pancake over.*)
 12) Who can *flip the pancake over* by using **just one hand? You
    must** catch it using the same hand, keeping the palm up!
 13) This time try to *flip the pancake over* by using 2 hands, but quickly
    turn your hands over and catch it on the top of your hands.
 14) Can you toss the bean bag back and forth (from hand
    to hand) across your body like a circus juggler?
 15) Try placing the bean bag on top of one foot, then swing your
    foot upward and see if you can catch the bean bag in the air.
 16) See if you can perform this same stunt using the other foot.
 17) Place the bean bag on top of your head. Now see if you can nod
    your head forward and catch the bean bag in front of your body.
 18) This time place the bean bag on top of your head, tilt your head back
    and attempt to catch the bean bag in back of your body.
 19) Can anyone in this class toss the bean bag up above his or her head
    and, without using hands, catch it on top of his or her head?
 20) Find other ways of tossing and catching **your bean bag.**

Lesson 2   STATION ◁1▷ LOW AND HIGH WALKING BOARDS   5th Week

PERFORMANCE OBJECTIVES
 By walking backwards on low board, and by walking forward on a high board while balancing bean bags on top
 of hands, student demonstrates dynamic balance, tactile and kinesthetic awareness and laterality.

(2)

24

EQUIPMENT
Low and high walking boards, 2 bean bags and mats.

CHALLENGES
1) *LOW BOARD* - Walk backwards to end of board.
2) *HIGH BOARD* - Walk forward carrying a bean bag on *top* of each hand. (Palms down.)

STRESS: Student "feels" for board with toes and then allows heels to come down when
walking backwards. Student does *not* turn head or slide feet.

Lesson 2   STATION ◇2◇ MAT STUNTS   5th Week

PERFORMANCE OBJECTIVES
By *frog jumping* and *log rolling*, student demonstrates laterality, kinesthetic and tactile stimulation, body
awareness and agility.

EQUIPMENT
Mats and rubber ball.

CHALLENGES
1) *FROG JUMP* - Starting position is sitting on heels (squatting), with hands placed flat
   on mat inside of legs, with knees outward. Student pushes from toes and springs from
   mat with hands leaving mat slightly ahead of feet. Student lands in squat position
   on feet.
2) *LOG ROLL* - In starting position student lays across mat on stomach, with body straight.
   Hands and arms may be kept at sides of body, or hands are clasped together out in
   front of head. Shoulders, hips, and knees move together in coordination, and
   body rolls over like a log down the center of the mats. (For alternate *log roll*
   challenge, ask student to hold rubber ball in hands as *log roll* is performed.)

STRESS: *FROG JUMP* - Arms are kept straight with hands close together.
        Take-off and landing on front part of feet near toes. *LOG ROLL* -
        The hips direct movement. Legs and arms are kept straight.

Lesson 2   STATION ◇3◇ SCOOTER BOARD WITH OBSTACLE   5th Week

PERFORMANCE OBJECTIVES
By moving on a scooter board around an obstacle, student demonstrates
bilateral coordination, balance, and kinesthetic awareness.

EQUIPMENT
Scooter board, traffic cone or bowling pin.

CHALLENGES
1) Student takes prone position (stomach) on scooter board, and uses hands and arms
   to propel scooter board around traffic cone and back to starting position.
2) Student takes kneeling position on scooter board and attempts the same challenge again.

STRESS: Body is balanced on scooter board--feet do not touch floor, and
        hands and arms work in rhythmic coordination.

PERFORMANCE OBJECTIVES
   By jumping from a jump box into a tire,
   and moving through the tire and cross
   bar pattern, student demonstrates locomotor skill, dynamic balance, foot-
   eye coordination, and space awareness.

EQUIPMENT
   Jump box with incline board, 4 bike
   tires (one of them red), cross bar
   and mats.

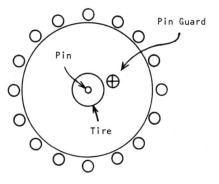

(3)

CHALLENGES
   1) Jump from box, land in red tire,
      and then continue *jumping* into tires, over cross bar, etc. (Use mats.)
   2) Jump from box, land in red tire, and then *hop* through the pattern.
   3) Jump *sideways* from box and land in tire, and then jump
      through the pattern moving *sideways*.
   4) Hop from box, land on one foot in red tire and continue *hopping* through the pattern.

STRESS: Controlled "soft" landing in red tires. Use of arms to help lift body. Modify
         height of cross bar on *hopping* challenge for successful performance.

Lesson 3   GAME - *CIRCLE-PIN THROW BALL*   5th & 6th Week

PERFORMANCE OBJECTIVES
   By performing in the *Circle-Pin Throw Ball* game, student demonstrates throwing at a target for accuracy.

EQUIPMENT
   Bowling pin, bike tire, and
   2 balls for each game.

DIRECTIONS
   1) A bowling pin is placed in the center of a
      circle, and is positioned inside a bike
      tire which serves as a restraining zone.
   2) One student is selected to be the pin guard,
      and tries to protect the pin from being
      knocked over by a thrown ball.
   3) Other class members are lined up around the
      outside of the circle and attempt to throw 2
      balls at the pin and knock it down.
   4) Any student who knocks the pin down becomes the new pin guard. The
      old pin guard takes this student's place on the outside of the circle.
   5) The pin guard cannot step inside the tire in attempting to
      protect the pin. He must move quickly, and is allowed to use
      hands, feet, or any part of the body to block the ball.

TEACHING SUGGESTIONS
   1) After the students understand the game, it is best
      to organize 2 games for more active involvement.
   2) Use 2 balls in each game so that play moves faster.
   3) If students are throwing too high, you may wish to
      have them pitch the ball underhand at the pin.
   4) Encourage passing the ball to players in order to catch the guard out of position.

(13)

PERFORMANCE OBJECTIVES
By performing the following challenges, student demonstrates ability in ball throwing and catching with
partner, and striking ball using hands with partner.

EQUIPMENT
Classroom set of rubber balls.

TEACHING SUGGESTIONS
1) Each participant should be paired up with a partner.
2) Each pair of partners should have a 7" diameter
   rubber ball in their possession to practice the skills. Distance between partners
   varies according to the skills to be practiced. Teacher must exercise good judgment
   on spacing.

CHALLENGES
1) Can you roll the ball back and forth with your partner by using 2 hands?
2) Who can roll the ball accurately to their partner by using one hand? Make sure
   you step towards your partner by using the opposite foot from your throwing hand.
3) Show me how you can toss the ball with 2 hands to your partner
   by using an *underhand* throw. (If students do not understand
   the term *underhand*, you might have to explain and demonstrate.)
4) Now toss and catch *underhand* with your partner by using one hand to "pitch" the ball.
5) This time, let's try a high *underhand* toss to your partner. Did you form
   a pocket with your hands and fingers to properly catch the ball?
6) Who can make an *overhand* throw to their partner by using 2 hands? We call
   this a *chest pass*. Bring the ball into your chest and push it forward!
7) Let's try the *chest pass* again by getting your thumbs in closer
   together and keeping your fingers spread on the ball.
8) Can you make an *overhand* toss to your partner by using just one hand?
9) Show me how you can bounce the ball to your partner by
   using 2 hands. This is called a *bounce pass*.
10) Now try the *bounce pass* again, but try to push the ball, *not*
    throw it down. Hands must be placed behind the ball!
11) Who can make a *bounce pass* to their partner by using only one hand?
12) Find another way of throwing and catching the ball with your partner.
13) I would like to see if you can drop the ball on the ground, and then hit it to
    your partner by using both hands. Make sure you strike it with your fingers!
14) How many times can you tap the ball back and forth with your fingers without
    a miss? Try to let the ball bounce only once between you and your partner.
15) Can you drop and hit the ball to your partner by using
    only one hand? (Use fingers and palm.)
16) Show me how you can drop the ball (let it bounce), and hit it to your
    partner by using a closed hand (fist).
17) Who can serve (hit) the ball out of their hand to their partner
    by using a closed hand *without* letting the ball bounce?
18) Is there some other way that you can strike the ball with your fingers so
    that your partner can catch it? (Toss ball up and volley it to partner.)

Lesson 2   STATION ◁1▷ LOW AND HIGH WALKING BOARDS   6th Week

PERFORMANCE OBJECTIVES
By walking backwards on a low board while stepping over bean bags and turning, and by
walking sideways on a high board, student demonstrates dynamic balance, tactile and
kinesthetic awareness, and laterality.

EQUIPMENT
Low and high walking boards, 2 bean bags and mats.

CHALLENGES
1) *LOW BOARD* - Walk *backwards*, step over first bean bag, make a complete turn at center of board, continue to walk backwards and step over 2nd bean bag.
2) *HIGH BOARD* - Walk *sideways* leading with right foot to end of board, and then return back to starting position leading with the left foot.

STRESS: *LOW BOARD* - Student "feels" for board and bean bag with toes, and does not turn head to look where going when moving backwards. Feet do not cross when moving sideways.

Lesson 2   STATION ◇2◇ OBSTACLE COURSE   6th Week

PERFORMANCE OBJECTIVES
By moving *under, through, over,* and *into* obstacle pattern, student demonstrates space awareness, directionality, body image, and locomotor coordination.

EQUIPMENT
Car tire with holder, 2 cross bars, red bike tire and mats.

CHALLENGES
1) Student crawls under low cross bar.
2) Student goes through auto tire.
3) Student *hops* over cross bar (weight on one foot).
4) Student lands in red tire and catches weight on one foot.
5) After each student has had the opportunity of 2 or more successful repetitions with the directed tasks, challenge student to find a different way of moving through obstacles.

STRESS: Controlled movements! Student attempts to relate to obstacles without touching with body.

Lesson 2   STATION ◇3◇ COORDINATION LADDER   6th Week

PERFORMANCE OBJECTIVES
By jumping and hopping, and moving along a coordination ladder, student demonstrates locomotor coordination, space awareness, dynamic balance, and motor planning ability.

EQUIPMENT
Coordination ladder and mats.

CHALLENGES
1) Jump sideways between rungs of ladder placed on mats or rug.
2) Hop on one foot between rungs of ladder.
3) *Frog jump* between rungs of ladder.
4) Find a different way of traveling to the end of the ladder with complete control over movements.

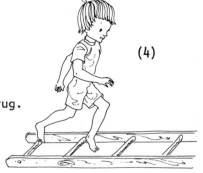

STRESS: Keep feet close together on sideways jumping. Slow and controlled
movements on hopping. Heels close together on *frog jump*.

Lesson 2   STATION ◁4▷ REBOUNDER   6th Week

PERFORMANCE OBJECTIVES
By jogging on a rebounder, student demonstrates locomotor control and laterality.

EQUIPMENT
Rebounder and mats.

(1)

(2)

CHALLENGES
1) *KNEE SLAP JOGGING* - Student stands over center area of
   rebounder with hands extended out in front of body.
   Student jogs (light running) with high knee action
   which results in slapping action against extended hands.
2) *CROSS-LATERAL JOGGING* - Student jogs over center area of rebounder using cross lateral limb movements. That is, raising
   left arm with right leg and raising right arm with left leg.

STRESS: Feet are placed approximately shoulder distance apart to
begin all jogging challenges. Eyes focus on instructor,
not down at feet. *CROSS LATERAL JOGGING* - Arms move in
opposition to leg movement. *FOR SAFETY* - It is advisable
to use "spotters" (position students) around the rebounder.
If mats are available, place on sides of rebounder for added safety.

===

Lesson 1   MOVEMENT EXPLORATION WITHOUT EQUIPMENT   7th Week

PERFORMANCE OBJECTIVES
By performing the following challenges, student
demonstrates space awareness and body awareness.

(9)

EQUIPMENT
No equipment needed except a whistle.

TEACHING SUGGESTIONS
1) At the beginning of the lesson, the teacher should establish boundary limits within which
   all movement will take place. A multi-purpose game court painted on the playground makes
   a good area for movement challenges.
2) An important part of this lesson is the development of body and space awareness which
   means the emphasis is placed on directing body movements without any collisions. The
   students should develop an awareness of their own "personal" space as well as "common"
   space which is shared by all students.

CHALLENGES
1) Walk until you hear the whistle. When you hear the whistle, freeze until the
   whistle is blown again.
2) This time when you hear the whistle, begin walking and look for big empty
   spaces to go to. Change directions each time you hear the whistle.
3) Who can walk by placing the heel of one foot against the toes of the other foot?
4) Try walking very low within the court area (common space) and then when you
   hear the whistle, see how tall you can walk.
5) Show me how high you can jump within your space.
6) Now look for a large empty space and see how far out into space you can jump.
   This is called a *long jump*.
7) Can you move by using 4 body parts in contact with the ground?
8) Who can move by using only one body part in contact

with the ground? (This is a hopping exercise.)
9) Show me how you can balance your body by using 3 body parts within your own personal space.
10) Can you find 3 new or different body parts to balance on?
11) Who can build a long narrow bridge by using their body? Now make this into a very short bridge.
12) How would you make a "draw-bridge"?
13) Try building a bridge by using just one foot and one hand in contact with the ground.
14) I would like to see how small or tiny you can make yourself.
15) Now slowly change into something very large.
16) Who can stretch like a rubber band?
17) How would you twist your body like a pretzel?
18) Show me how you would shake your body out like a dust mop.
19) Can you move about the "common" space like a bouncing ball without touching anyone?
20) This time show me how quickly you can move about the "common" space, but when you hear the whistle, stop low to the ground.

Lesson 2   STATION <1> LOW AND HIGH WALKING BOARDS   7th Week

PERFORMANCE OBJECTIVES
   By walking over a cross bar and through the hoop on a low board, and by walking forward and sideways on a high board, student demonstrates dynamic balance, directionality, laterality, and visual-motor coordination.

EQUIPMENT
   Low and high walking boards, cross bar, hoop, and mats.

CHALLENGES
  1) *LOW BOARD* - Walk forward, step over cross bar, make a full turn at center of board, go through hoop, and walk to end of board. (Hoop must be held up by an aide.)
  2) *HIGH BOARD* - Walk forward 1/3rd of the way, walk sideways 1/3rd of the way, and then walk backward to the end of the board.

STRESS: *LOW BOARD* - Make turn slowly at center of board, and then attempt to move through hoop without touching it.

Lesson 2   STATION <2> MAT STUNTS   7th Week

PERFORMANCE OBJECTIVES
   By *rabbit hopping* and performing a *lay out*, student demonstrates bilateral coordination, body awareness, and tactile-kinesthetic stimulation.

EQUIPMENT
   Mats.

CHALLENGES
  1) *LAY OUT* - Students kneel across mat with arms extended under shoulders, hands flat on mat, and knees under hips. On auditory signal (whistle or hand clap) students all *lay out* flat on the mat with palms of hands slapping mat. This is a reaction drill in which students change levels of body positioning. All students at this station perform stunt at the same time.
  2) *RABBIT HOP* - Starting position is squatting with hands placed flat on mat and knees together *between* arms. Student reaches forward with hands to begin movement and then jumps feet up to hands. This pattern is maintained with hands moving ahead of feet.

30

STRESS: *LAY OUT* - Hands break fall with body extended forward. A good starting position
is important. *RABBIT HOP* - Knees and feet are kept together.
Hands move first followed by feet.

Lesson 2   STATION ◁3▷ JUMP BOX   7th Week

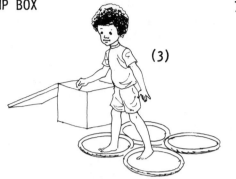
(3)

PERFORMANCE OBJECTIVES
By jumping from jump box and performing
mid-air quarter turns and landing in tires,
student demonstrates dynamic balance, body
awareness, and space awareness.

EQUIPMENT
Jump box with incline board, four
bike tires, and mats.

CHALLENGES
1) Walk up incline board onto jump box, take good jumping position, jump and perform
quarter turn while airborne, and land facing in challenged
direction either quarter turn left or quarter turn right.
2) Students able to perform task in challenge (1) with good control,
may be permitted to run up incline board and perform same task.
3) Place 4 tires on mat and challenge students to perform quarter
turn to left or right with feet landing in correct tires.

STRESS: Student jumps out away from box and does not twist (turn) body until after
forward jump is made. *FOR SAFETY* - Make sure mats are used to land on.

Lesson 2   STATION ◁4▷ REBOUND NET AND LAUNCHING BOARD   7th Week

PERFORMANCE OBJECTIVES
By throwing and catching, and launching and
catching bean bags with the use of rebound
net and launching board, student demonstrates
hand-eye coordination and foot-eye coordination.

EQUIPMENT
Rebound net, launching board
and classroom set of bean bags.

CHALLENGES
1) *REBOUND NET* - Overhand throwing, and
catching with 2 hands forming a pocket.
Student steps toward target (net) with
opposite foot from throwing hand.
2) *LAUNCHING BOARD* - Step on board with preferred foot, launch, eye track, and catch bag.

STRESS: Student should be given 5 to 10 trials on each turn at both the net and launcher.
Student attempts to catch the bean bag 5 to 10 times in succession. Student successful with 2 hands should be challenged to catch with each hand individually.
Hands form pocket with fingers spread to properly catch bag. Eyes direct hands as
a unit to the bag. A "soft" throw is made so that rebound speed from net is reduced.

Lesson 3   GAME - *ONE-TWO-THREE*   7th & 8th Week

PERFORMANCE OBJECTIVES
By performing in the *One-Two-Three* game, student demonstrates listening
skills, locomotor (transport) skills, and space awareness.

31

EQUIPMENT
   Whistle.

DIRECTIONS
   1) Class should be divided into 4 equal groups
      with each group assigned to line up on one
      side of a rectangular court area. (One group
      is on each side of the court to begin play.)
   2) When the teacher blows the whistle *once*, all
      students standing on the end lines move to
      the opposite end line. (They exchange
      places.) This would be groups 1 and 2 in
      the diagram.
   3) When the teacher blows the whistle *twice*,
      all students standing on the side-lines
      move to the opposite side-line.
      (Exchange places.)

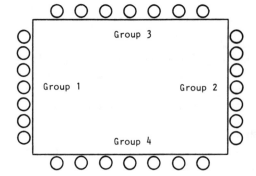

   4) When the teacher blows the whistle *three* times, all students change to the *opposite* line.
   5) Before blowing the whistle, the teacher should challenge the students to move
      with a definite locomotor skill. (Running, jumping, skipping, etc.)
   6) Any students who: a) move when it is *not* their whistle signal;
      b) use the wrong movement skill; or c) collide with another
      student; are eliminated and line up at a designated spot.
   7) Usually it is best to keep them out of the game for only a short
      period of time. A good rule is to allow one player to return
      to his side once another player has been eliminated.

TEACHING SUGGESTIONS
   1) Multi-purpose game courts painted on playgrounds make a good game area.
   2) Use a wide variety of movement skills.
   3) Ball skills may be worked into this game with each student having a
      ball in his or her possession.

Lesson 1   MOVEMENT EXPLORATION WITH ROPES   8th Week

PERFORMANCE OBJECTIVES
   By performing the following challenges, student demonstrates recognition and creation of basic geometric shapes, numbers, and letters.

EQUIPMENT
   Classroom set of jump ropes.

(14)

TEACHING SUGGESTIONS
   1) Each student should have a rope in his or
      her possession to begin the lesson.
   2) Adequate space for movement must
      be allowed between participants.

CHALLENGES
   1) Who can make a circle with their rope placed on the ground?
   2) Can you jump into the center of your circle and then jump back out again?
   3) Can you jump in and out of your circle 5 times without stopping?
   4) How would you travel around the outside of your circle while balancing
      on one hand in the center of your circle? (Called a *coffee grinder*.)
   5) Show me how you would make a square with your rope?
   6) I would like to see if you can perform a *balance walk* around the top of your square by
      touching the heel of one foot against the toes of the other. (Student walks on the rope.)
   7) How many sides does a square have? While balancing on
      one foot, who can hop 4 times in and out of their square?

8) Can you make a number 4 inside of your square by using your body parts?
9) This time I would like to see you make a triangle with
   your rope. How many sides does your triangle have?
10) See if you can jump all the way around your triangle using only 3 jumps.
11) How would you balance with 3 body parts touching inside of your triangle?
12) Who can shape their rope into a number 3?
13) Now add 5 to this number and show me your answer by using your rope.
14) Can you stand with one foot inside each end of your 8?
15) Find a way of jumping into the air and changing the position of your feet.
16) Subtract 2 from your number 8 and show me the answer by using your rope.
17) How would you make your number 6 into a 9 without moving the rope?
18) Now subtract 4 from the number 9 and form your rope into the answer.
19) Who can hop around their number 5 by using just 5 hops, but
    each time you hop, land on the opposite side of the rope?
20) This time, see if you can make the 3rd letter of the alphabet with your rope.
21) Can you walk your "C" like a cat by keeping the rope between your hands and feet?
22) What other letters of the alphabet can you make by using your rope?

Lesson 2   STATION ◁1▷ COORDINATION LADDER   8th Week

PERFORMANCE OBJECTIVES
  By *balance walking* and *rabbit hopping* along
  a coordination ladder, student demonstrates
  dynamic balance, laterality, space awareness, and motor planning ability.

EQUIPMENT
  Coordination ladder and mats.

CHALLENGES
  1) *BALANCE WALK* - Student performs a *balance walk* on *side rails* of ladder placed on mats or
     rug. (Student walks down one side of ladder and returns back to
     starting position on other side of ladder.)
  2) *RABBIT HOP* - Student performs a *rabbit hop* between and over rungs of the ladder
     placed on mats or rug. Hands may be placed on sides or rungs of ladder for bet-
     ter control of movement while feet travel over and land between rungs of ladder.

STRESS: *BALANCE WALK* - Use of arms to help make adjustments in center of gravity while
        walking on sides of ladder. Slow movements! *RABBIT HOP* - Student
        may place hands wherever he feels most successful, but feet
        stay close together and land in spaces between rungs.

Lesson 2   STATION ◁2▷ BALL DRIBBLING WITH HOOPS   8th Week

PERFORMANCE OBJECTIVES
  By dribbling a ball through a hoop pattern, student
  demonstrates hand-eye coordination, memory sequencing ability, and basic locomotor skill.

EQUIPMENT
  Ball and 5 hoops.

CHALLENGES
  1) Student holds ball, jumps into each hoop, and
     dribbles ball a directed number of times in-
     side each hoop. (Students with poor hand-eye coordination who are obviously
     not able to achieve success with a dribble may be permitted to use a bounce and catch.)

STRESS: Student should verbalize the number of dribbles in each hoop. Student *jumps*

33

from hoop to hoop with both feet leaving floor at same time. Finger tips control ball on dribble with a push ("soft" fingers), and not a slapping action.

Lesson 2   STATION ◇3◇ REBOUNDER   8th Week

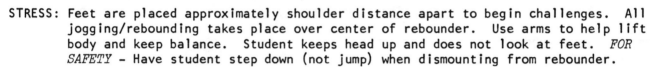
(2)

PERFORMANCE OBJECTIVES
   By rebounding (jumping) on a rebounder and "freezing" on command, student demonstrates dynamic balance, body awareness, and locomotor control.

EQUIPMENT
   Rebounder and mats.

CHALLENGES
   1) *REVIEW: CROSS-LATERAL JOGGING* - Student jogs (light running) over rebounder center. On command of "freeze", student stops in place.
   2) *CONTROLLED REBOUNDING* - Student jumps (rebounds) 5-10 times to get the "feel" of it. Student keeps body straight and does not lean forward. On command of "freeze", student stops with slightly bent knees.

STRESS: Feet are placed approximately shoulder distance apart to begin challenges. All jogging/rebounding takes place over center of rebounder. Use arms to help lift body and keep balance. Student keeps head up and does not look at feet. *FOR SAFETY* - Have student step down (not jump) when dismounting from rebounder.

Lesson 2   STATION ◇4◇ JUMPING AND HOPPING WITH OBSTACLES   8th Week

PERFORMANCE OBJECTIVES
   By jumping through a tire and cross bar pattern, and by hopping through a rope and tire pattern, student demonstrates locomotor control, balance, space aware- ness, and eye-foot coordination.

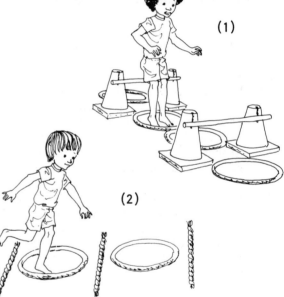
(1)

EQUIPMENT
   Two cross bars, 4 jump ropes, and 7 bike tires (2 of them red).

CHALLENGES
   1) *PATTERN 1* - Student jumps into tire, over first cross bar, *stops* in red tire, jumps into tire, over 2nd cross bar and then *stops* in 2nd red tire.
   2) *PATTERN 2* - Student hops over rope (brook) and lands in first tire and then continues hopping through the pattern. (Over, into, over, into, etc.) This is called *cross the brook*.

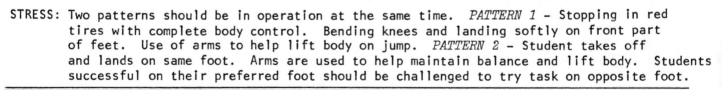
(2)

STRESS: Two patterns should be in operation at the same time. *PATTERN 1* - Stopping in red tires with complete body control. Bending knees and landing softly on front part of feet. Use of arms to help lift body on jump. *PATTERN 2* - Student takes off and lands on same foot. Arms are used to help maintain balance and lift body. Students successful on their preferred foot should be challenged to try task on opposite foot.

Lesson 1   MOVEMENT EXPLORATION WITH HOOPS   9th Week

PERFORMANCE OBJECTIVES
   By performing the following challenges, student demonstrates hand-eye and foot-eye coordination, and space awareness.

EQUIPMENT
Classroom set of hoops.

TEACHING SUGGESTIONS
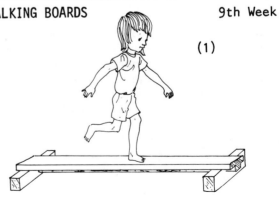

(5)

1) All participants should have a hoop in their possession to begin the lesson.
2) Students are asked to select their own personal space to work in. Stress that much space is needed between participants because they will be rolling, and tossing, and catching their hoops.

CHALLENGES
1) How high can you stretch (reach) with the hoop held in both hands?
2) Holding the hoop up high above your head, pretend that you are driving a car around a curvy mountain road. How far around to your right and your left can you turn and twist the hoop?
3) Who can spin their hoop like an egg beater? This is an electric egg beater which means that once you turn on the power, it must turn by itself.
4) This time try spinning your hoop like an egg beater, but before your hoop stops spinning see if you can jump in and out of it without stopping the hoop. (Students should let the hoop spin low to the ground before attempting to jump in and out.)
5) Show me how you would use your hoop like a jump rope.
6) Is there another way you could jump your hoop?
7) When I blow the whistle (or clap hands) show me how quickly you can move in and out of your hoop. (Student holds hoop in front of body.)
8) Who can throw their hoop in the air and catch it before it lands without moving their feet?
9) Now pretend that you are a famous magician. How would you throw your hoop out on the ground so that it will roll back to you?
10) Try making it come back to you again, but before it arrives back see if you can go through your hoop without touching it.
11) Being careful not to bump into anyone, can you roll your hoop forward and keep it from falling over?
12) While your hoop is rolling, can you run around it without touching the hoop?
13) Show me how you can find your original space, and stand in it holding your hoop.
14) Face a person near you whom you would like to work with as a partner.
15) See if you can exchange hoops with your partner by rolling them back and forth. Can you catch the hoop in one hand and roll it with the other? (Place hand flat on top of hoop to make it roll smoothly.)
16) Would one partner please raise one hand? I would like the person with their hand raised to give their hoop to their partner so that one person has two hoops.
17) Now show me how you can make an obstacle course by using both hoops held in different positions. When I blow the whistle the other partners will see how many times they can go in and out of the obstacle course without touching either hoop. Stop when the whistle blows again.
18) Give the hoops to your partner and see if he or she can make a different obstacle course. When the whistle blows, show me how many times you can go in and out without touching.

Lesson 2   STATION ◁1▷ LOW AND HIGH WALKING BOARDS   9th Week

PERFORMANCE OBJECTIVES
By balancing and turning on one foot on the low board, and by carrying a ball on the high board, student demonstrates balance, tactile and kinesthetic awareness, and laterality.

(1)

EQUIPMENT
Low and high walking boards, ball, and mats.

CHALLENGES
  1) *LOW BOARD* - Walk forward to center of board, balance on one foot, make ½
     turn while balancing on this same foot and walk backwards to end of board.
  2) *HIGH BOARD* - Walk forward to end of board carrying a
     7" rubber ball out in front of body.

STRESS: Head up, eyes looking straight ahead and *not* down at feet. In-
        structor may wish to hold hand up at eye level for visual focusing.

Lesson 2   STATION ◇2◇ MAT STUNTS WITH OBSTACLES   9th Week

PERFORMANCE OBJECTIVES
  By *alligator crawling* under cross bar obstacles, and by *frog jumping* over cross
  bar obstacles, student demonstrates laterality, directionality, space awareness,
  and motor planning ability.

EQUIPMENT
  Mats and 2 cross bars.

CHALLENGES
  1) *ALLIGATOR CRAWL* - Perform *alligator crawl*
     on stomach down length of mats, crawling
     under 2 cross bars evenly spaced on mats.
  2) *FROG JUMP* - Perform *frog jump* down length
     of mats, jumping over 2 cross bars evenly spaced on mats. (Check
     5th Week, Lesson 2, Station 2, for correct body position on *frog jump*.)

STRESS: *ALLIGATOR CRAWL* - Use of both arms and legs in coordination to transport
        body forward. Student goes under bars without touching with body.
        FROG JUMP - Student must motor plan movements so that body lands
        proper distance from cross bar enabling a successful jump over bar.

Lesson 2   STATION ◇3◇ JUMP BOX   9th Week

PERFORMANCE OBJECTIVES
  By jumping from jump box and performing
  a half turn, then landing in tires, student demonstrates dynamic balance, foot-
  eye coordination, and space awareness.

EQUIPMENT
  Jump box with incline board,
  2 bike tires, and mats.

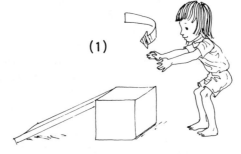

CHALLENGES
  1) Walk up incline board onto jump box, take correct jumping position, jump and perform
     a ½ turn while airborne. Land facing *towards jump box* with good balance and control.
  2) Students able to perform task as in (1) with good control
     may run up incline board and perform the same task.
  3) Place 2 tires side by side on mat and challenge student to perform
     jump with ½ turn and land with one foot inside of each tire.

STRESS: Student jumps out away from box and does not twist (turn) body until after
        forward jump is made. *FOR SAFETY* - Make sure mats are used to land on.

Lesson 2   STATION ◁4▷ REBOUND NET AND LAUNCHING BOARD   9th Week

PERFORMANCE OBJECTIVES
By throwing and catching bean bags with one
hand with rebound net, and by launching and
clapping hands, etc., before catching bean
bags from launching board, student demonstrates laterality and hand-eye coordination.

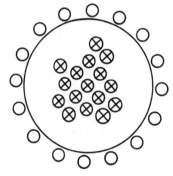

EQUIPMENT
Rebound net, launching board
and classroom set of bean bags.

CHALLENGES
1) *REBOUND NET* - Students who can consistently throw and catch a bean bag using 2 hands
should be challenged to catch the bag using only one hand. If able to catch using only
their dominant or preferred hand, then allow them to experiment using the opposite hand.
Allow 10 trials per turn. Insist on concentrated and purposeful performance.
2) *LAUNCHING BOARD* - Challenge student to try the following tasks:
a) Launch bean bag, clap hands and catch it; b) Launch bag, snap
fingers and catch it; c) Launch bag, slap knees and catch it. Allow
10 trials per turn. Student may attempt to catch bag with one or 2 hands.

STRESS: *REBOUND NET* - Student should be aggressive in catching style. Hand or hands go out to
meet the bean bag. Fingers must be relaxed--not stiff or tense. *LAUNCHING BOARD* -
The higher the object is launched, the more time available to complete task. Heel
contacts board. Hands move under bean bag to form catching pocket with palms up.

Lesson 3   GAME - *TEAM DODGEBALL*   9th & 10th Week

PERFORMANCE OBJECTIVES
By performing in the *Team Dodgeball* game, student demonstrates throwing for accuracy and dodging skills.

EQUIPMENT
Two balls.

DIRECTIONS
1) Two equal teams of players are selected with
one team "A" in the center of the circle, and
the other team "B" lined up around the outside
of the circle to begin play.
2) Team "B" has 2 balls in their possession which they will use to hit players on team "A".
3) A game is divided up into 2 time periods of 5 minutes each.
4) The object of the game is to see which team can eliminate (hit) the
most players on the opposing team with a 5 minute time period.
5) In order to be eliminated, a player must be hit below the waist with the ball.
6) A player hit below the waist must leave the inside of the circle and stand
in a designated "prison zone" until the 5 minute time period is up.
7) At the end of the 5 minute time period, team "B" would receive one
point for each player on team "A" captured in their prison.
8) The teams now change places with team "A" moving to the outside of the circle and team
"B" moving about the inside of the circle. A new 5 minute time period is started.
9) The team hitting (capturing) the most opposing players within a
5 minute time period would be declared the winner of the game.
10) After a team winner has been declared, it is fun to have all the players not hit (captured) from both teams inside the circle and all other players from both teams around

the outside of the circle. Competition is now centered around who will be the individual class champion. The last player eliminated is declared "Class Champion".

TEACHING SUGGESTIONS
1) Encourage quick throwing of the balls using an underhand throw for better control and safety.
2) When having a "play-off" at the end to determine the individual champion, allow
   players eliminated to join the rest of the players around the outside of the circle.
3) Accurate timing is important to allow both teams an equal amount of time inside the circle.

| Lesson 1 | MOVEMENT EXPLORATION WITH RHYTHM STICKS | 10th Week |

PERFORMANCE OBJECTIVES   (9)
   By performing the following challenges, student demonstrates finger
dexterity (manipulation), and hand-eye coordination reaction.

EQUIPMENT
   Classroom set of rhythm sticks.

TEACHING SUGGESTIONS
1) Each participant should have one rhythm stick
   in his or her possession to begin the lesson.
2) Adequate spacing is important to the success of the lesson.
3) For good control, it is necessary to have a definite signal which participants understand to mean *stop activity and listen!* (For example: Hold stick up above your head
   as a signal for everyone to hold his or her stick up, or use the traditional whistle.)

CHALLENGES
1) Holding your stick in one hand, show me how you can make your fingers crawl up and down
   the tree (stick). (Fingers start at the bottom of the stick and climb up to the top.)
2) Now do it again by using your other hand.
3) Can you hold your stick in one hand (horizontally) and make your fingers
   roll it forward and then backwards like riding on top of a log?
   Try keeping your fingers on the center of the log.
4) Who can twirl their stick in and out of their fingers like
   twirling a baton? Now change hands and try it again.
5) How fast can you make your stick spin around while resting on the floor or ground?
6) See how quickly you can pass the stick around your body from hand
   to hand. When I give a signal, stop and quickly change direction.
7) Can you pass your stick from hand to hand by moving it in and out your legs and around your
   knees in a figure-8 pattern? When I give a signal, stop and quickly change direction.
8) Hold your stick horizontally in front of your body with one hand
   on each end. I would like to see how many of you can step over
   the stick with each foot without releasing the ends of the stick.
9) Who can hold the stick vertically in one hand up above their head
   level, then release the stick and reach across their body with the
   opposite hand and catch it before it hits the ground?
10) Now reverse hands and try this same challenge.
11) This time try holding your stick in front of your body at eye level (hori-
    zontally) with one hand at each end. Your challenge is to release the stick
    and try to catch it by using only one hand before the stick hits the ground.
    (Palm of catching hand should be facing downward.)
12) Show me how you can toss your stick from hand to hand without dropping it.
13) As you toss your stick from hand to hand try making just your eyes
    follow the stick without any head movement. (Head is stationary.)
14) See if you can lift the stick up, then release it above your
    head level and catch it above your head by using the *same* hand.
15) How many of you can successfully perform this same skill by using the other hand?

PERFORMANCE OBJECTIVES
By performing a *swan balance* in 2 tires on a low board, and by bouncing and catching a ball over a tire target on a high board, student demonstrates balance, laterality, and hand-eye coordination.

EQUIPMENT
Low and high walking boards, 3 bike tires, ball, and mats.

CHALLENGES
1) *LOW BOARD* - Walk forward, perform a *swan balance* on left foot in first tire, continue walking to 2nd tire and perform a *swan balance* on the right foot.
2) *HIGH BOARD* - Walk forward to middle of high board carrying a 7" rubber ball, bounce and catch ball in bike tire placed on floor, and continue walking to the end of the board.

STRESS: *LOW BOARD* - On *swan balance* student bends forward from waist, extends arms out sideways, and holds balance on one foot. *HIGH BOARD* - Ball is pushed downward to bounce in tire, not just a dropping action. Eyes focus on tire and then the ball!

PERFORMANCE OBJECTIVES
By moving along a coordination ladder touching various body parts, student demonstrates body awareness, laterality, dynamic balance, and tactile-kinesthetic stimulation.

EQUIPMENT
Coordination ladder and mats.

CHALLENGES
1) Can you travel down the ladder using only 2 body parts (or 2 points of contact)?
2) Can you move on the ladder using just 3 body parts?
3) How would you move down the ladder using 4 body parts (or 4 points of contact)?

STRESS: Student creates own pattern of movement and attempts different types of movement when responding to verbal problem. Speed is *not* important, but body control is!

PERFORMANCE OBJECTIVES
By jumping and hopping over a combination rope, tire, and cross bar pattern, student demonstrates locomotor coordination, balance, and laterality.

EQUIPMENT
Cross bar, 4 bike tires, and 2 jump ropes.

CHALLENGES
1) Starting inside of first tire, *hop* back and forth over rope which is tied between 2 tires until reaching the 2nd tire.
2) *Jump* from 2nd tire over cross bar and land inside of 3rd tire.
3) Continue *hopping* back and forth over rope until reaching final tire. (Challenge student to use opposite foot from starting foot.)

STRESS: Using first the right foot and then the left foot for hopping practice on each side of the body. Student should stop with complete control and balance inside each tire. Student should *not* lean forward while hopping--shoulders are back and head upright.

Lesson 2   STATION ◁4▷ REBOUNDER   10th Week

PERFORMANCE OBJECTIVES
By performing straddle jumps on a rebounder, student demonstrates body awareness, bilateral control, and dynamic balance.

EQUIPMENT
Rebounder and mats.

(2)

CHALLENGES
1) *REVIEW: CONTROLLED REBOUNDING* - Student rebounds (jumps) over the center area of the rebounder 5-10 times. On the command of "freeze" student stops in place by letting knees give slightly.
2) *STRADDLE JUMPS* - Student starts with feet close together over center point of rebounder. Hands are placed on hips. Student rebounds (jumps) with feet moving apart out to sides and then back to starting position. Student repeats this same movement sequence in a series of 5-10 straddle jumps.

STRESS: Keep head up and shoulders back maintaining good body alignment. Body position must be maintained over center point of rebounder.
STRADDLE JUMPS - Both feet must move sideward and return at same time on straddle jump. Practice on floor before performing on rebounder.

Lesson 1   MOVEMENT EXPLORATION WITH PARACHUTE   11th Week

PERFORMANCE OBJECTIVES
By performing the following challenges, student demonstrates teamwork and listening skills, and upper body strength.

EQUIPMENT
Classroom-size parachute and 3 rubber balls.

(2d)

TEACHING SUGGESTIONS
1) The parachute may be used indoors or outdoors, but is easier to use indoors if space is available. The wind factors when used outdoors sometimes make it difficult to perform certain stunts.
2) For good control students should be spaced evenly around the chute using an overhand grip (palms down).
3) In order to secure a firmer grip on the parachute, it is advisable to have students roll the edge of the chute 5 to 10 rolls (depends on design and size of chute) towards the center. This also makes the canopy smaller and easier to control.
4) Adapt problem solving prefaces such as "Can you...?", "Show me how you can...", etc., to the challenges.

CHALLENGES

1) *REVIEW* the following challenges from the 4th Week Lesson:
   a) *OCEAN WAVES* - (Shake the parachute up and down.)
   b) *INFLATION (UMBRELLA)* - (Parachute is lifted up over heads to inflate and then back down.)
   c) *TENTING* - (Students inflate parachute and walk forward 3 steps with arms raised high.)
   d) *IGLOO (HIDE-A-WAY)* - (Students inflate parachute and then seal themselves inside.)
   e) *POPCORN* - (Students shake parachute up and down and attempt to pop 3 rubber balls up into the air.)

2) Try the following *NEW* challenges:
   a) *SMALL MUSHROOM* - hold the parachute tight and on command quickly bend down and seal it against the ground. Air is captured inside the parachute.
   b) *LARGE MUSHROOM* - lift the parachute up over your heads and on command take one step forward and seal it down against the ground.
   c) *PASS THE PARACHUTE* - grip the parachute and pull it tight. On command everyone start passing it around in a circle without moving your feet. Quick movement of hands is important! (Have students change direction on signal from whistle.)
   d) *PARACHUTE MARCHING* - all grip the parachute with the same hand (right or left) and on command begin marching around in a circle. (March music makes it more fun!)
   e) *PARACHUTE JOGGING* - grip the chute with one hand and jog around in a circle. Change directions on command!

Lesson 2   STATION ◇1◇ LOW AND HIGH WALKING BOARDS   11th Week

PERFORMANCE OBJECTIVES
   By bouncing and catching a ball on the low board, and by walking sideways and turning on the high board, student demonstrates dynamic balance, hand-eye coordination and laterality.

EQUIPMENT
   Low and high walking boards, ball, and mats.

CHALLENGES
   1) *LOW BOARD* - Walk forward carrying a 7" ball, bounce and catch the ball after every 2 steps.
   2) *HIGH BOARD* - Walk sideways to center of board with left foot leading, make a ½ turn, and walk sideways to end of board with right foot leading.

STRESS: *LOW BOARD* - Pushing ball down to bounce it on floor not just dropping ball. Eyes focus on ball! *HIGH BOARD* - Feet do *not* cross when walking sideways.

Lesson 2   STATION ◇2◇ MAT STUNTS   11th Week

PERFORMANCE OBJECTIVES
   By *egg rolling* and performing a *forward roll*, student demonstrates body awareness, tactile and kinesthetic stimulation, and balance.

EQUIPMENT
   Mats.

41

CHALLENGES

1) *EGG ROLL* – Student starts in kneeling position with arms crossed and elbows resting on mat. Student rolls over across shoulders and back moving sideways and returns to starting position.

2) *FORWARD ROLL* – Start in squat position (sitting on heels) with hands flat on mat, knees together inside of arms. Students can be reminded that this is also the starting position for the *rabbit hop*. Next, ask student to tuck chin against knees, then raise hips up slightly, push with toes, lower back of head to mat, and roll over keeping tucked (round position) like a ball. (Have students practice basic positioning by using verbal cues "tuck chin", "lift hips". They must acquire feeling of hips leading the body over with the head staying tucked.)

STRESS: *EGG ROLL* – The knees are pulled in tight toward chest as student rolls across back. Arms stay crossed throughout the roll and legs do not untuck. *FORWARD ROLL* – Hands are flat on mat for solid support and do *not* move forward as roll is started. Toes are placed up to edge of mat for starting position. *Top* of head does *not* touch mat on roll.

Lesson 2   STATION ◁3▷ JUMP BOX WITH OBSTACLE COURSE   11th Week

PERFORMANCE OBJECTIVES

By jumping from a jump box and moving over, into, under, and through an obstacle pattern, student demonstrates body and space awareness, directionality, and locomotor coordination.

(2)

EQUIPMENT

Jump box with incline board, 2 cross bars, bike tire, car tire with holder, and mats.

CHALLENGES

1) Student jumps from box over cross bar and lands inside of tire.
2) Student crawls under low cross bar.
3) Student crawls through auto tire.
4) After a couple of trials, challenge students to move through the course in a different way.

STRESS: Landing in bike tire with complete body control, and moving under bar and through car tire without touching obstacles. *FOR SAFETY* – Use mats under obstacle course.

Lesson 2   STATION ◁4▷ REBOUNDER   11th Week

PERFORMANCE OBJECTIVES

By performing quarter turns while rebounding on rebounder, student demonstrates directionality, body awareness, and dynamic balance.

EQUIPMENT

Rebounder and mats.

(2)

CHALLENGES

1) *REVIEW: STRADDLE JUMPS* – Student rebounds (jumps) with feet moving apart sidewards and then back together. Hands are placed on hips. Student performs a series of 5-10 straddle jumps while maintaining good body control.

2) *QUARTER TURNS* – Student rebounds (jumps) 2 times and then turns (twists) body a quarter turn to the right. Student uses the rhythmic count "1-2-turn", and maintains this rhythm. Student continues rebounding 2 times and turning (twisting) one quarter of the way each time until returning to starting position.

STRESS: *QUARTER TURNS* – 4 quarter turns will return student to starting position. Arms help turn body. All turns take place in mid-air over rebounder center. Do *not* look at feet. Feet stay about shoulder distance apart on each turn. (Teacher may wish to help "cue" performer by verbalizing rhythmic count "1-2-turn", etc.)

PERFORMANCE OBJECTIVES
   By performing in the *Out Ball* game, student demonstrates
   ball handling (passing and catching), and
   listening (alertness) skills.

EQUIPMENT
   Whistle and 2 balls.

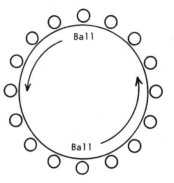

DIRECTIONS
  1) Have class form around a large circle on the play-
     ground with 2 balls available for passing and catch-
     ing. (Balls may be the same or different sizes.)
  2) The balls should be on opposite halves
     of the circle to begin the game.
  3) On a whistle signal to begin, the balls are passed
     from student to student around the
     circle using an underhand pass.
  4) Whenever the teacher blows the whistle, the 2 players holding a ball in their hands re-
     ceive an "O" (first letter in the word "OUT") against them. The game then continues.
  5) Once players have received an "OUT" against them, they must step
     into the center of the circle ("The Witches Pot").
  6) This player (or players) must stay in the center of the circle until another player (or
     players) have received an "OUT" against them. They would then exchange places, and the
     player (or players) going back to the circle would start free with no letters against them.
  7) Each player must handle the balls in turn as they are passed around the circle,
     and when the whistle blows they must hold the ball, if in their possession.

TEACHING SUGGESTIONS
  1) Have both balls passed to the right or counter-clockwise.
  2) Encourage students to turn to their left after passing the ball so
     that they are ready to catch the next ball when it is passed to them.
  3) Hands must form a pocket and be ready to catch the ball.
  4) With 2 balls in action, the game moves fast and is rather suspenseful for students.

Lesson 1   MOVEMENT EXPLORATION WITH BALLS   12th Week

PERFORMANCE OBJECTIVES
   By performing the following challenges, student demonstrates dribbling
   the ball (using fingers to continously push the ball
   down without catching it).

EQUIPMENT
   Classroom set of rubber balls.

(2)

TEACHING SUGGESTIONS
  1) Each participant should have a ball in his
     or her possession to begin the lesson.
  2) A "scatter" formation within a designated area is used with
     each student standing in his or her own "personal" space.
  3) Emphasize on the dribble that the ball is pushed down with fingers
     spread and finger tips controlling the ball. Use "soft" fingers!

CHALLENGES
  1) Can you dribble the ball by using 2 hands?
  2) Who can dribble the ball in place by using just one hand?
  3) How low can you dribble the ball?
  4) Can you dribble the ball high without losing control?

5) Show me how you would dribble the ball between low and high.
6) This time dribble the ball by using just your right hand.
7) Now try dribbling the ball by using just your left hand.
8) Who can dribble the ball 5 times by using their right hand and then 5 times by using their left hand?
9) Can you alternate (change) hands on each dribble by using first the right hand and then the left hand?
10) Try balancing on one foot and dribble the ball.
11) I would like to see if anyone can dribble the ball and then slowly sit down without stopping their dribble.
12) Now can you stand back up and still keep dribbling the ball?
13) Focus on my hand and dribble the ball without looking down. Try keeping your hand close to the ball.
14) Who can dribble the ball with their eyes closed? Your finger tips must "feel" the ball!
15) Show me how you can dribble the ball under each leg without stopping your dribble.
16) Find other body parts to dribble the ball with. (Elbows, head, etc.)
17) Now try walking forward and backward by dribbling the ball with just one hand.
18) This time keep your eyes on my hands. If my hands move forward, dribble the ball moving forward. If my hands move backward, dribble the ball moving backwards.
19) Now we are going to dribble the ball as we move about within our area and look for big spaces to move into. If I blow the whistle (or clap hands) stop in place, but do *not* stop your dribble! When the whistle blows again, continue to move about and dribble the ball.
20) For a final challenge, see how many different ways you can think of to dribble your ball.

Lesson 2   STATION ◁1▷ LOW AND HIGH WALKING BOARDS   12th Week

PERFORMANCE OBJECTIVES
By picking up bean bag and placing on head and making a ½ turn on low board, and by tossing and catching a ball with instructor on high board, student demonstrates dynamic balance, tactile and kinesthetic awareness, and hand-eye coordination.

(1)

(2)

EQUIPMENT
Low and high walking boards, rubber ball, bean bag, and mats.

CHALLENGES
1) *LOW BOARD* - Walk forward to center of board, pick up bean bag and place on head, make a ½ turn, and walk backward to end of board.
2) *HIGH BOARD* - Walk forward carrying a rubber ball, toss and catch with instructor.

STRESS: *LOW BOARD* - Student lowers body down to pick up bean bag (not bending from waist). Student does not slide feet or turn head when walking backwards. *HIGH BOARD* - Student tosses and catches ball after every few steps using an underhand toss.

Lesson 2   STATION ◁2▷ SCOOTER BOARD WITH OBSTACLES   12th Week

(1)

PERFORMANCE OBJECTIVES
By moving on a scooter board under a cross bar pattern, student demonstrates locomotor coordination, balance, space awareness, and directionality.

EQUIPMENT
Scooter board and 2 cross bars.

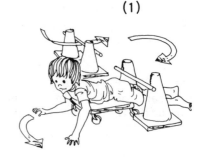

44

CHALLENGES

1) Student assumes prone (stomach) position on scooter board, and using hands in alternate movements travels around the obstacles and under the cross bars as illustrated. (Cross bars should be in straight line as shown in illustration.)

STRESS: Student attempts to go under cross bars and around cones without touching.

Lesson 2   STATION ◇3◇ REBOUNDER   12th Week

PERFORMANCE OBJECTIVES
By performing half turns while rebounding on a rebounder, student demonstrates directionality, body awareness, and dynamic balance.

EQUIPMENT
Rebounder and mats.

CHALLENGES

1) *REVIEW: QUARTER TURNS* - Student rebounds 2 times and then turns (twists) body a quarter turn to the right. (Cue is "1-2-turn", etc.) Student continues this same pattern until starting position is reached again.

2) *HALF TURNS* - Student rebounds (jumps) 2 times and then while airborne turns (twists) body a half turn to the right so that student lands facing in the opposite direction. Student repeats pattern again to get back to starting position. A series of half turns can be done using the count "1-2-turn". Student trys to maintain this basic rhythm pattern.

(2)

STRESS: Turn or twist body at the height of the rebound. Keep a shoulder's distance apart and over center area of rebounder. Do *not* watch feet! Teacher may wish to "cue" the performer at first by verbalizing the count "1-2-turn", etc.

Lesson 2   STATION ◇4◇ REBOUND NET AND LAUNCHING BOARD   12th Week

PERFORMANCE OBJECTIVES
By throwing and clapping hands, etc., before catching from rebound net, and by launching and catching 2 bean bags from a launching board, student demonstrates laterality and hand-eye coordination.

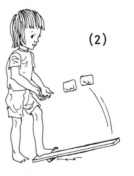

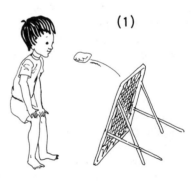

(2)   (1)

EQUIPMENT
Classroom set of bean bags, rebound net and launching board.

CHALLENGES

1) *REBOUND NET* - Student is challenged to throw a bean bag (or tennis ball) against the net and perform the following tasks: a) Clap hands and catch bean bag; b) Snap fingers and catch bag; c) Slap knees and catch bag; d) Touch toes and catch bag (much more difficult task).

2) *LAUNCHING BOARD* - Students able to catch bean bag in each hand individually should be challenged to launch and catch 2 bags. Bean bags are placed side by side across the bord (not on top of each other). Use 2 different colored bags, if available. Student should catch lowest bag first.

STRESS: *REBOUND NET* - Eyes watch (follow) bean bag into hands which move out to meet the bag. Hands must work together as a catching unit. Body positioning in front of bag is important to success. *LAUNCHING BOARD* - Hands are cupped forming pocket under lowest bag first and then move to 2nd bean bag. More skillful students can try guiding one hand to each bean bag.

45

PERFORMANCE OBJECTIVES
     By performing the following challenges, stu-
     dent demonstrates balance and locomotor skills.

(7)

EQUIPMENT
     Classroom set of bean bags.

TEACHING SUGGESTIONS
   1) All participants should have a bean bag
      in their possession to begin the lesson.
   2) Students are in a "scatter" formation on the playground (or indoors if space is avail-
      able). There should be enough space allowed between participants so that they
      do not interfere with each other's performance.
   3) A whistle is helpful for class control.

CHALLENGES
   1) Who can balance the bean bag on top of their head, then slowly
      sit down without dropping the bean bag off their head?
   2) Now see if you can stand back up with the bean bag still balanced on your head.
   3) With the bean bag balanced on your head, try rotating your head in as large
      a circle as possible without moving your feet or dropping the bean bag.
   4) Let's see if you can balance your bean bag on top of other body parts.
      Chin? Right shoulder? Left wrist? Right knee? Left foot?
   5) With the bean bag still balanced on your left foot, can you swing your left leg forward and
      back keeping the bean bag in place? Now try this same challenge using your right foot.
   6) Can you hold the bean bag in your left hand with your arm extended straight forward, then
      kick your right foot up to touch your outstretched hand without losing your balance?
   7) Try balancing the bean bag on your left knee, then hop
      forward a few hops without dropping the bean bag.
   8) Show me how you would move like a crab (inverted body position)
      with the bean bag balanced on your stomach area.
   9) With the bean bag placed on the ground (or floor) see if you
      can balance on top of your bean bag using one leg only.
  10) While still balancing on this same leg, see how low you
      can go to the ground without losing your balance.

We are now going to try many different challenges with the bean bag resting on the ground.
   1) Can you discover at least 5 different ways of moving from one
      side of your bag to the other side without touching it?
   2) Try jumping forward and backward over your bean bag.
   3) Show me how quickly you can jump back and forth over your bean bag by moving *sideways*.
   4) Who can hop forward and backward over the bean bag without losing their
      balance? Remember a hop means you are moving on *one foot only*.
   5) This time show me how you can balance with one hand resting on the bean bag.
      In this same position, see how quickly you can move around your bean bag.
   6) As a final challenge, I would like to see how many different body parts you can dis-
      cover to use in picking your bean bag off the ground (or floor). Hands do not count.

PERFORMANCE OBJECTIVES
     By performing combination straddle jumps and quarter turns on a rebounder,
     student demonstrates body awareness, bilateral control, and dynamic balance.

EQUIPMENT
     Rebounder and mats.

CHALLENGES
  1) *REVIEW: HALF TURNS* - Student rebounds 2 times and while airborne
     performs a half turn to the right. Student repeats same pattern
     to reach starting position. (2 half turns brings student to
     starting position.) Also have student perform half turns to left.
  2) *COMBINATION STRADDLE JUMPS AND QUARTER TURNS* - Student starts
     with feet close together over center of rebounder and hands
     placed on hips. 2 straddle jumps are performed with feet mov-
     ing apart out to sides and then back to starting position on
     both jumps, followed by a quarter turn to the right. This same
     sequence continues until student returns to starting position.

(2)

STRESS: Keep head up and shoulders back maintaining good body alignment.
        COMBINATION STRADDLE JUMPS AND QUARTER TURNS - 4 quarter turns
        will return student to starting position. Teacher may wish to
        have students practice on floor before performing on rebounder.

Lesson 2   STATION ◇2◇ COORDINATION LADDER   13th Week

PERFORMANCE OBJECTIVES
  By moving along a coordination ladder while
  bouncing and catching a ball, student demonstrates hand-eye coordination, balance,
  space awareness, and tactile stimulation.

EQUIPMENT
  Coordination ladder and rubber ball.

CHALLENGES
  1) Walk on side rails of ladder, bounce
     and catch the ball once in each of the spaces between the rungs.
  2) Walk on *rungs* of ladder, bounce and catch ball in spaces between rungs.
  3) Students ready for more difficult task can be challenged to toss
     and catch ball while walking on the rungs of the ladder.

STRESS: Slow movements while walking on ladder. Ball is pushed down
        into spacial target, not just dropped. Hands form pocket to
        catch ball using "soft" fingers. Finger tips control ball.

Lesson 2   STATION ◇3◇ MAT STUNTS   13th Week

PERFORMANCE OBJECTIVES
  By *forward rolling*, and performing a *forward roll to standing position*, student
  demonstrates body awareness, gross-motor
  coordination, and dynamic balance.

EQUIPMENT
  Mats.

(2)

CHALLENGES
  1) *REVIEW: FORWARD ROLL* - Squat position,
     sitting on heels, knees between arms, hands flat on mat. Verbal cues:
     "tuck chin", "lift hips", and "roll". See 11th Week, Lesson 2, Station 2.
  2) *FORWARD ROLL TO STANDING POSITION* - Student starts at end of mat in
     standing position (attention). Student squats, performs *forward roll*,
     and comes right back up to standing position. This is followed by 2
     repetitions of the same stunt for a complete series of 3 rolls.

STRESS: *REVIEW: FORWARD ROLL* - A good starting position before each roll is made and keeping "tucked" through-out the roll. *FORWARD ROLL TO STANDING POSITION* - Student comes up to position of "attention" before beginning each roll on the series of 3.

Lesson 2   STATION ◁4▷ JUMPING AND HOPPING WITH OBSTACLES   13th Week

PERFORMANCE OBJECTIVES
   By jumping and hopping through a cross bar and tire pattern, student demonstrates directionality, space awareness, locomotor skill, balance, and kinesthetic stimulation.

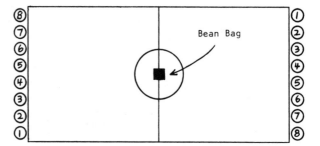

(1)

EQUIPMENT
   Three cross bars and 4 bike tires (one of them red).

CHALLENGES
   1) Student *jumps* over cross bar and lands in red tire followed by a series of long jumps into tires, over bar, etc. Distance between cross bar and tires depends on ability level of participants. (For variations on jumping task, change distance between obstacles and also height of cross bars.)
   2) Place obstacles in closer together and challenge students to *hop* the pattern.

STRESS: Bending of knees on take off and landing. Use of arm thrust to help lift and propel body forward. "Soft" landing on "balls" of feet with full body control. *Adjustment of body position in air before landing so that body faces next target (obstacle).*

Lesson 3   GAME - *STEAL THE BACON*   13th & 14th Week

PERFORMANCE OBJECTIVES
   By performing in the *Steal The Bacon* game, student demonstrates quickness of movement (agility), and tagging (without pushing) skills.

EQUIPMENT
   Bean bag and optional bike tire.

DIRECTIONS
   1) Two equal teams line up on opposite sides of a court about 20 to 30 feet apart.
   2) A bean bag (or similar object) is placed in the center of the playing space between the 2 lines. (You may wish to use a bike tire as a restraining area into which the bean bag is placed.)
   3) Each student is given a number. (Numbers must correspond on each team.) Best to have boys with similar numbers and girls with similar numbers.
   4) The leader calls a number, and the 2 players assigned that number go after the bacon (bean bag).
   5) The student who first picks up the object attempts to run back across his team's goal line without being tagged by the opponent.
   6) One point is scored for each player who successfully returns across his team's goal line with the bacon without being tagged. *Optional Rule:* Player who successfully tags player with bacon scores one point.
   7) Team scoring the most points is the winner.

TEACHING SUGGESTIONS
   1) If 2 players arrive at the bacon at the same time, encourage them to circle around the bacon and attempt to catch the opponent off guard before grabbing it.

2) If possible, organize the activity so that 2 games are going on at once using the same court. Use 2 bean bags with 2 opposing teams competing for one bacon and 2 opposing teams for the 2nd bacon.

| Lesson 1 | MOVEMENT EXPLORATION WITH ROPES | 14th Week |

PERFORMANCE OBJECTIVES
By performing the following challenges, student demonstrates rope turning, and jumping and hopping.

(9)

EQUIPMENT
Classroom set of jump ropes.

TEACHING SUGGESTIONS
1) Each student should have a rope in his or her possession to begin the lesson.
2) Establish a system of distributing and collecting the ropes.
3) Adequate space for movement must be allowed between participants.
4) Students must listen to the entire challenge before starting to move.

CHALLENGES
1) Holding both ends of your rope in your right hand, show me how you can turn the rope forward so that the rope (loop) hits the ground next to your foot. Try keeping your arm down and use plenty of wrist action.
2) Can you turn the rope backwards using this same hand and make it hit the ground?
3) Now hold both ends of your rope in your left hand and turn it forward. Try turning it backwards.
4) Who can make their rope turn circles in front of their body and strike the ground? Try turning it to the right (clockwise) and then to the left (counter-clockwise). Can you change hands and perform this stunt?
5) Turning your rope over your head, show me how a helicopter would look. Can you perform this task using your other hand?
6) While turning your rope over your head, can you change hands without stopping or dropping the rope? Change hands several times.
7) We are now going to practice turning and jumping the rope at the same time. (This synchronization is important for arms and legs to develop needed coordination for regular rope jumping.) Using your right hand, can you turn the rope on one side of your body and *jump* in rhythm as the rope hits the ground near your foot? Now change hands and repeat this same challenge.
8) Who can *hop* on their right foot while turning the rope forward by using their left hand?
9) This time, see if you can *hop* on your left foot while turning the rope forward with your right hand.
10) I would like each of you to face a partner. Would one partner please raise his or her hand. The students with hands raised should give their rope to their partner so that one person has a rope in each hand. While holding a rope in each hand by its ends, try turning *both* ropes forward at the same time and make them hit the ground at the sides of your feet. Remember, that strong wrist action is important in turning your rope!
11) Show me how you can turn *both* ropes and jump in rhythm as the ropes hit the ground near your feet. See if your partner can jump in time with your jumping and rope turning.
12) Now give the ropes to your partner and let him or her practice turning the 2 ropes forward at the sides of the body. Practice jumping in time with your partner turning the ropes.
13) While holding your rope with both hands (one end in each hand) see if you can jump the rope while you swing it back and forth under your feet, but *not* over your head. This is called *blue bells*.
14) As a final challenge, I would like to see how many of you can turn the rope over your head and jump it. How many times can you jump it without stopping the rope?

PERFORMANCE OBJECTIVES
   By bouncing and catching a ball from rebound in tire along a low board, and by touching knees to bean bags on the high board, student demonstrates balance, laterality, directionality, and hand-eye coordination.

EQUIPMENT
   Low and high walking boards, rubber ball, 4 bike tires, 2 bean bags, and mats.

CHALLENGES
   1) *LOW BOARD* - Walk forward carrying a rubber ball, bounce and catch ball in 4 bike tires placed on alternate (right tire, left tire, right tire, left tire) sides of the board. (Tires are placed on the floor close to the board.)
   2) *HIGH BOARD* - Walk forward, touch right knee to first bean bag on board, continue walking forward and touch left knee to 2nd bean bag. (Bean bags are spaced approximately 4 feet apart on the walking board.)

STRESS: *LOW BOARD* - Feet do not turn sideways as ball is bounced in tires. Ball is pushed down into tire openings not just dropped. For added challenge have student verbalize left or right as ball is bounced into tire. *HIGH BOARD* - Head and upper body area is held straight as knee is lowered to bean bag. Head and shoulders do *not* lean forward. Student has to step over bean bag with forward foot and plan corrct positioning of rear foot for knee to contact bean bag. (This is a difficult task.)

PERFORMANCE OBJECTIVES
   By performing twister jumps on a rebounder, student demonstrates locomotor control and dynamic balance.

EQUIPMENT
   Rebounder and mats.

CHALLENGES
   1) *REVIEW: COMBINATION STRADDLE JUMPS AND QUARTER TURNS* - Student rebounds performing 2 straddle jumps (feet move sideward and back together) followed by a quarter turn to the right. Sequence is repeated 4 times which brings student back to starting position.
   2) *TWISTER JUMPS* - Student rebounds and twists body at the waist with head and shoulders facing straight ahead. The direction of the twist alternates with toes pointing toward the left, then the right, etc. A rhythmic rebounding action is maintained as twists are performed.

STRESS: *TWISTER JUMPS* - Shoulders remain straight and back with good posture and feet are close together as twists are performed. The waist and hips lead the twisting action. Arms remain in relaxed position at side of body with elbows bent and hands carried in forward position. Arms help to maintain body balance and do not change basic position as twist is performed.

Lesson 2   STATION ◁3▷ JUMP BOX   14th Week

PERFORMANCE OBJECTIVES
By clapping hands and grabbing a ball while jumping from a
jump box, student demonstrates dynamic balance, hand-
eye coordination, body awareness, and agility.

CHALLENGES
EQUIPMENT
Jump box with incline board, ball, and mats.

CHALLENGES
1) Student jumps from box, claps hands
   over head, and lands with good balance.
2) Student performs same challenge as in (1)
   only starts with a *run* up the incline board.
3) Student *walks* up incline board and takes
   correct jumping position on box. Student
   jumps from box and grabs ball held up high in front of box by the instructor. (Ball
   is held in one hand extended out in front of jumper. Student grabs the ball held
   stationary by the instructor and lands with the ball clutched in both hands. Ball must
   be held at a level and distance where the student must jump out and up to reach the ball.

STRESS: *1)* – Student attempts to get arms back down near sides of body after hand
         clapping to help accomplish a controlled landing. *3)* – Student focuses
         on the ball and attempts to grasp the ball at the height of the jump.

(1)

Lesson 2   STATION ◁4▷ OBSTACLE COURSE   14th Week

PERFORMANCE OBJECTIVES
By moving under, through, and over an obstacle course, student demonstrates directionality, space awareness, and locomotor control.

EQUIPMENT
Car tire with holder, 2 cross bars and a mat.

CHALLENGES
1) Student crawls under cross bar without touching.
2) Student goes through tire without touching.
3) Student rolls over cross bar by using a *forward roll*.
4) After a few trials, challenge students to find new ways of moving through obstacle course.

STRESS: On *forward roll*, student takes standing position close to cross bar, reaches over
        bar, places hands flat on mat, then pushes off with feet, tucks head and body,
        and rolls over. *FOR SAFETY* – Be sure to use mat under cross bar on *forward roll*.

(2)

Lesson 1   MOVEMENT EXPLORATION WITH HOOPS AND BALLS   15th Week

PERFORMANCE OBJECTIVES
By performing the following challenges, student demonstrates skill
in tossing and catching ball, dribbling ball, and space awareness.

EQUIPMENT
Classroom set of hoops and balls.

TEACHING SUGGESTIONS
1) All participants should have a hoop and a
   ball in their possession to begin the lesson.

(11)

2) Each student is asked to select their own "personal" space to work in and to allow plenty of space between hoops so that there will be no collisions.
3) Student stands inside of hoop, holding ball and awaits verbal challenges as presented by instructor. The hoop serves to confine and refine basic ball skills and adds space awareness to the challenges as presented.

CHALLENGES
1) Keeping your body inside your hoop, can you toss and catch your ball?
2) Without leaving your hoop, can you toss the ball up and above your head, clap your hands and catch the ball?
3) Who can toss their ball up high, turn completely around and catch the ball? Remember, you must stay inside of your hoop!
4) Show me how you can walk around your hoop by keeping one foot on the inside and one foot on the outside and toss and catch your ball.
5) When I blow the whistle (or clap hands), change directions by moving backwards and perform this same challenge.
6) This time try this same challenge, but see if you can clap hands and catch the ball every 2 steps.
7) I would like to see how many of you can dribble the ball inside your hoop without losing control. Remember, a dribble means to continually push the ball down without stopping or catching it!
8) Can you dribble the ball inside your hoop by constantly changing hands? (Left, right, etc.)
9) This time, by keeping your feet *inside* the hoop, try to dribble the ball around the *outside* of your hoop.
10) If I blow the whistle (or clap hands), see if you can change hands and change direction without stopping your dribble.
11) Who can walk around the *outside* of their hoop, but dribble the ball in the *center* of their hoop? Try to keep the ball right in the middle of your hoop.
12) When I blow the whistle, you must change hands and change directions without stopping your dribble.
13) Now, placing the ball on the ground inside your hoop, see how quickly you can roll the ball around your legs transferring it from hand to hand. Make your fingers control the ball!
14) Can you roll the ball in and out of your legs in a figure-8 pattern by using your fingers?
15) Show me how you can use only your feet to move the ball around the *inside* of your hoop. (Try using the sides of your feet, for the most part.)
16) As a final challenge, see if you can discover a way of using your ball and hoop at the same time involving any parts of your body. The ball and hoop both must be moving at the same time with control.

Lesson 2   STATION ◁1▷ REBOUNDER   15th Week

PERFORMANCE OBJECTIVES
By performing lateral jumps on a rebounder, student demonstrates body awareness, bilateral control, and dynamic balance.

EQUIPMENT
Rebounder and mats.

(2)

CHALLENGES
1) *REVIEW: TWISTER JUMPS* - Student rebounds and twists body at the waist with toes alternately pointing to the left, then the right, etc. Head, shoulders, and arms do *not* twist, only the lower body.
2) *LATERAL JUMPS* - Student starts with feet together over center point of rebounder. Hands are held in comfortable position to help balance body. Student rebounds

(jumps) in short sideward movements with feet and legs
staying together.

STRESS: *LATERAL JUMPS* - Must be "spotted" very carefully. Student can easily lose control. Feet stay together and move as one unit in short sideward motions back
and forth. Have students practice on floor before performing on rebounder.

Lesson 2   STATION ◇2◇ COORDINATION LADDER   15th Week

PERFORMANCE OBJECTIVES
By walking with bean bag on head, and by moving on all
4's along inclined coordination ladder, student demonstrates dynamic balance, tactile and kinesthetic
stimulation, foot-eye coordination, and space awareness.

EQUIPMENT
Coordination ladder, 2 intermediate walking board supports, and mats.

(1)

CHALLENGES
Attach 2 intermediate walking board supports under end
rung of ladder to place ladder in an incline position.
1) Walk forward on *rungs* of ladder while balancing bean bag on top of head. Upon reaching
   end supports, turn and walk forward back to starting position without dropping bean bag.
2) Walk forward on hands and feet (4-legged position) using hands on
   side rails and feet on rungs upon reaching end supports, return to
   starting position by moving *backwards* using a *4-legged walk*.
3) Challenge student to show you a different way of moving to the end of the ladder and back.

STRESS: *1) & 2)* - Slow movements with complete body control.
Feet are placed on rungs of ladder *not* sides.

Lesson 2   STATION ◇3◇ MAT STUNTS   15th Week

PERFORMANCE OBJECTIVES
By performing *curl-ups* and a *body aware-*
ness reaction drill, student demonstrates body image, abdominal strength,
kinesthetic awareness and agility.

EQUIPMENT
Mats.

(1)

CHALLENGES
1) *CURL-UP* - Student lays down on back across mat with body straight. (Legs are together with arms and hands at side of body.) Student sits up slowly reaching forward with arms straight and at the same time drawing knees up toward chest. (Knees
   are between arms.) Student returns slowly to starting position to complete *curl-up*.
   (Students should perform this stunt in a group of several students at same time with
   instructor giving cues: "up", "hold", "down". Perform 6 to 10 repetitions.
2) *BODY AWARENESS REACTION DRILL* - Students react to verbal challenges of instructor and
   quickly change body positions on mat. Examples: "front" (stomach), "back", "left side",
   "right side", "feet", "seat", "knees", etc. (Several students can do it at same time.)

STRESS: *CURL-UP* - Hands are *not* used to push off from mat. Arms and legs start movement
at the same time. Student grasps legs after reaching sitting position. *BODY*
AWARENESS REACTION DRILL - Quick movements are important but students do *not*
"throw" themselves onto the mat. Do *not* call "knees" when students are standing because tendency is to drop on knees. Proper spacing is important for safety.

PERFORMANCE OBJECTIVES
   By hopping through a combination rope and
hoop pattern, student demonstrates locomotor
coordination, laterality, and space awareness.

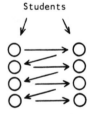

EQUIPMENT
   Six hoops and 4 ropes.

                                                 (1)

CHALLENGES
   If space is available, set up 2 patterns
as shown and have students alternate back
and forth between the 2 patterns.
                                                (2)
  1) *PATTERN 1* - Student is challenged to
     hop within spaces provided by hoops
     with ropes placed across the center
     and *under* the 3 hoops. Hop on right foot, then through on left foot.
  2) *PATTERN 2* - Student is challenged to *hop* in forward-sideways pattern with weight
     shifting to left or right foot depending on side of rope where body is positioned.
     Two hops may be required by some students to travel from hoop to hoop. (Place rope
     under hoops as shown.) Start pattern on right side with right foot leading movement.
     Then go through on left side with left foot leading movement.

STRESS: Balance and control maintained on one foot with soft, light movements. Shoulders
       are back, not leaning forward. Speed is *not* important, *control* is the focus!

═══

Lesson 3   GAME - *ZIGZAG DANISH ROUNDERS*   15th & 16th Week

PERFORMANCE OBJECTIVES
   By performing in the *Zigzag Danish Rounders* game, student demonstrates
ball handling (passing and catching), and quickness of movement skills.

                                              Students

EQUIPMENT
   Four balls and a whistle.

DIRECTIONS
  1) Students are organized into 4 teams of approximately 6 students to a team. (May have 7 or
     8 students on a team, if necessary, but each team should have an equal number of students.)
  2) Students on each team line up so that 3 are facing 3
     (or 4 facing 3, etc.) as shown in the diagram.
  3) Each team has one ball in its possession to begin the game.
  4) On a signal to begin play, students on each team begin passing their ball back
     and forth in a zigzag pattern *down the line and back* within their group.
  5) The teacher should designate the type of pass to be used before start-
     ing play, and should offer brief instruction in proper skill technique.
  6) When the whistle is blown, the student on each team with the ball in his or her
     possession holds it up over his or her head and all *other* members of the team quickly
     line up behind this student. *Emphasize that student with ball remains stationary.*
  7) After *all* team members are in a straight line, the ball is handed over-
     head from student to student until reaching the last student in line.
  8) Each student in line must handle the ball, and it must be *handed* from student to student,
     not thrown. If the ball is dropped, it is picked up and passed on from that point.
  9) Upon receiving the ball, the last student in line runs up to the head of
     his line. All students quickly squat down, and yell out "Danish Rounders".
 10) The first team finishing correctly and calling out "Danish Rounders" wins one point.
 11) The teams now line up again in starting formation and the game continues
     as before. The teacher may wish to change the type of pass used.
 12) The team scoring the most points at the conclusion of playing time, wins the game.

TEACHING SUGGESTIONS
1) Be sure to vary the types of passes used. Examples: underhand pass, overhand pass, bounce pass, etc.
2) You may also wish to vary the way the ball is handed down the line from student to student. Examples: overhead, under and between legs, and alternate over-under method.
3) Stress to students that they take their time and make accurate passes using correct skill and technique. (Gripping ball correctly with fingers spread, stepping forward slightly ahead of pass, following through, etc.)
4) Stress that speed is not important until the whistle blows to line up behind the student holding the ball.
5) In order to get students thinking about and practicing correct skill, it is recommended that the teacher occasionally penalize a team finishing first by not awarding them a point. This is done when very poor technique is demonstrated by team members even though finishing first.
6) This is an outstanding ball handling skill development game. Everyone is active and the skill can be focused on without undue pressure of winning.

Lesson 1   MOVEMENT EXPLORATION WITH RHYTHM STICKS   16th Week

(14)

PERFORMANCE OBJECTIVES
By performing the following challenges, student demonstrates balance, body awareness, and hand-eye skills.

EQUIPMENT
Classroom set of rhythm sticks.

TEACHING SUGGESTIONS
1) Each participant should have *one* rhythm stick in their possession to begin the lesson.
2) Make sure that adequate spacing is present before starting the lesson.
3) For good control, it is vital that a definite signal be used and understood for starting and stopping movement challenges.
4) Participants who cannot exercise self-control may be asked to turn in their stick and observe activity until ready to observe rules of conduct.

CHALLENGES
1) Who can balance the stick on top of their head (horizontally) without having it roll off?
2) Can you stand on one foot only, and still balance the stick on top of your head?
3) Let's discover other body parts on which we can balance our stick. Show me how you can balance it on your forehead. Nose? Chin? Right shoulder? Left knee? Right foot? (And so on.)
4) Now try balancing your stick on 4 fingers. 3 fingers? 2 fingers?
5) Can anyone balance their stick on just one finger?
6) How many of you can place the stick across the fingers of both hands, and then make it roll across your arms to the shoulder area and back down to your fingers?
7) Holding your stick by its ends by using the middle finger of each hand, see if you can place the stick down on the ground without bending your knees.
8) With the stick resting on the ground in front of you, can you hop over and back on one foot without losing your balance?
9) Standing with one foot on each side of your stick (stick parallel to feet), show me how you can jump into the air and perform a *half turn* and then land with one foot on each side of the stick. (Student lands facing in opposite direction from starting point.)
10) Can you jump back to the starting position without losing your balance?
11) With your stick still resting on the ground, try building a long narrow bridge over the top of the stick by using 4 body parts to balance on.
12) Who can lower their bridge down to touch the stick and then raise it back up again?
13) Keeping your stick on the ground, see how many different body parts you can roll your stick with. Did anyone discover 10 or more body parts?
14) Holding your stick in one hand, can you flip it over one time only and catch it using the same hand. This is called *flip the pancake over.*

15) Now try changing hands. Flip it over with one hand and catch it with the other.
16) As a final challenge, balance the stick on top of your head, then let it
roll off the back of your head and catch it behind your body. (Hands
should catch stick down by the waist area, not up by the shoulders.)

Lesson 2   STATION <1> LOW AND HIGH WALKING BOARDS   16th Week

PERFORMANCE OBJECTIVES
   By walking on narrow side of low board, and by
   stepping over bean bags without looking at them
   on high board, student demonstrates balance,   (2)
   visual-motor coordination, laterality, and space awareness.

EQUIPMENT
   Low and high walking boards with 4 bean bags and mats.

CHALLENGES
   1) *LOW BOARD* - Place board in low supports
      so that 2" narrow walking surface is up. Student walks board forward,
      moving slowly, and attempts to maintain balance. (This is the first
      time the 2" walking surface has been used in the Lesson Plans.)
   2) *HIGH BOARD* - Use regular 4" walking surface and place 4 bean bags on the board
      spaced evenly apart. (Approximately 2 feet between each bean bag.) Student is
      challenged to walk board forward with hands on hips and stepping over bean
      bags without looking at feet. (Students able to perform task moving forward
      should be challenged to try it moving sideways and then moving backwards.)

STRESS: *LOW BOARD* - Walk board slowly using hands and arms to make necessary adjustments
              in center of gravity. Eyes focus on instructor's hand, not down at feet or board.
        HIGH BOARD - Student must plan movements so that feet do not touch bean bags.

Lesson 2   STATION <2> JUMP BOX WITH OBSTACLES   16th Week

PERFORMANCE OBJECTIVES
   By jumping off jump box, over cross bar,   (2)
   into tire, and *forward rolling* out, stu-
   dent demonstrates dynamic balance, body
   and space awareness, and kinesthetic stimulation.

EQUIPMENT
   Jump box with incline board, cross
   bar, red bike tire and mats.

CHALLENGES
   1) Student walks up incline board and takes correct jumping position on box. Student
      jumps over cross bar and lands in "red" tire with good body control.
   2) Same challenge as (1) only after landing in tire, student places hands
      on mat *outside* of tire and performs a *forward roll*.
   3) For students needing greater challenge, place cross bar and tire further distance
      from box. Safety must, however, always be considered in terms of task difficulty.

STRESS: Bending of knees upon landing to cushion body. On *forward roll*, feet are in the tire
        and hands placed outside of tire. Hips raise up and guide body over on roll with head
        coming under body in a tucked position. *FOR SAFETY* - Use mats to land and roll on.

PERFORMANCE OBJECTIVES
By over-hand throwing and catching bean bags from rebound net, and by catching bean bags in each hand at same time from launching board, student demonstrates laterality, and hand-eye coordination.

EQUIPMENT
Rebound net, launching board, and classroom set of bean bags.

CHALLENGES
1) *REBOUND NET* - Over-hand throwing and catching. Each student performs 10 over-hand throws and receives one point each time the bean bag is caught. Ten points is a perfect score.
2) *LAUNCHING BOARD* - Student launches 2 bean bags at same time, and attempts to catch one bag in each hand. Bags are placed side by side across end of board, *not* on top of each other. Use 2 different colored bean bags. One hand reacts to each bag with palm facing up. Students not ready for this can attempt easier task of cupping hands together and catching the bean bags.

STRESS: *REBOUND NET* - Eyes watch (follow) bean bag into hands. Hands work together as a catching unit and move out to meet the bean bag. *LAUNCHING BOARD* - Hands move individually to the bags with the palms up. One hand is visually guided under each bean bag.

PERFORMANCE OBJECTIVES
By performing side kicks on a rebounder, student demonstrates body awareness, locomotor control, and dynamic balance.

EQUIPMENT
Rebounder and mats.

CHALLENGES
1) *REVIEW: LATERAL JUMPS* - Student rebounds (jumps) in short sideward movements and performs a series of lateral jumps with feet and legs together.
2) *SIDE KICKS* - Student rebounds with weight shifting alternately from one foot to the other as the non-supporting leg kicks out sideward. Starting position is with weight supported over one foot and opposite foot and leg slightly out sideward.

STRESS: *SIDE KICKS* - Correct starting position with weight supported on one foot and leg over center area of rebounder. To begin movement, support (balance) leg kicks out sideward as non-support leg assumes support position. Movement sequence continues with rebounding and sideward leg alternating the kick from one foot to the other. A basic rhythm must be maintained.

PERFORMANCE OBJECTIVES
By performing the following challenges, student demonstrates body awareness, and hoop motion and control skills.

57

EQUIPMENT
Classroom set of hoops.

TEACHING SUGGESTIONS
1) All participants should have a hoop in their possession to begin the lesson.
2) Students are asked to select their own personal space to work in.
   Stress that enough space is needed between participants to allow
   for freedom of movement without interference or collisions.
3) Allow students adequate time and opportunities to explore each challenge or problem.

CHALLENGES
1) Show me how you can make your hoop spin around one arm.
2) Who can make their hoop travel up and down their arm while spinning around?
3) How would you change your hoop from one arm to the other without stopping it?
4) How fast can you make your hoop go while turning on your arm?
5) Try making your hoop go around your arm very slow without stopping.
6) Who can make their hoop turn circles around their neck?
7) This time see if you can make your hoop move around your hips (or waist).
   Try starting with the hoop resting against the back side of your body.
8) Can anyone make the hoop travel very fast around their hips,
   and then travel very slow without losing control?
9) Show me how you can make your hoop go from fast to slow, and then very fast again.
10) Is there anyone who can make their hoop turn circles around their knees?
11) This time, see if you can spin your hoop around your ankle.
12) How would you make your hoop travel down from your hips to your
   knees without losing control? This takes very good body control.
13) How low can you place your body and still keep your hoop moving? (Lowest
   would probably be lying on back with the hoop turning around an arm.)
14) Try making your hoop turn circles around your hips while walking forward.
15) Would each of you please turn and face a partner. We are now
   going to solve problems while working with our partner.
16) Using *one* hoop only, can you toss and catch the hoop with your partner without dropping it?
17) How many students can catch a hoop on one arm which has been thrown by their partner?
18) Can you catch it on this same arm and make it spin without stopping the hoop?
19) This time we are going to try and use *two* hoops with our partner. Can you toss and
   catch the hoops so that both hoops are moving at the same time? (Each partner starts with
   one hoop in his or her possession and they synchronize their tossing of the hoops.)
20) Find other ways of exchanging hoops with your partner.

Lesson 2   STATION ◇1◇ REBOUNDER   17th Week

PERFORMANCE OBJECTIVES
   By performing jumping jacks on a rebounder, student demonstrates
   bilateral control, body awareness, and dynamic balance.

EQUIPMENT
   Rebounder and mats.

(2)

CHALLENGES
1) *REVIEW: SIDE KICKS* - Student rebounds with weight shifting
   from one foot to the other as non-support leg kicks out sideways. Starting position is with weight supported over one foot.
2) *JUMPING JACKS* - Student starts with feet together over center point of rebounder
   and arms down at side. Student rebounds (jumps) with hands and arms moving out
   and up over head, as feet move out sideward. Hands, arms, and feet move back to
   starting position to complete one jumping jack. Student continues this coordinated
   rhythmic sequence between arms and legs, and performs a series of 5 jumping jacks.

STRESS: *JUMPING JACKS* - Arms and legs begin sideward movement at the same time, and then return to starting position at same time. Hands may be clapped together over head, but this is optional. Have students practice this task from a standing position on the floor before attempting it on the rebounder. Practice can be accomplished in small group formation.

Lesson 2   STATION ◁2▷ MAT STUNTS   17th Week

PERFORMANCE OBJECTIVES
   By *rabbit hopping* and performing a *rabbit hop - forward roll combination*, student demonstrates motor planning ability, tactile and kinesthetic stimulation, body awareness, and laterality.

(2)

EQUIPMENT
   Mats.

CHALLENGES
   1) *REVIEW: RABBIT HOP* - Briefly review the *rabbit hop* in preparation for Challenge (2).
      Starting position is squatting with hands placed flat on mat and knees together *between* arms. Student reaches forward with hands to begin movement and then jumps feet up to hands. This pattern is maintained with hands moving first, and then the feet.
   2) *RABBIT HOP FORWARD ROLL COMBINATION* - Student performs a *rabbit hop* followed by a *forward roll*. This same pattern continues until reaching the end of the mat.

STRESS: Good starting position (sitting on heels with knees together inside of arms) for both the *rabbit hop* and *forward roll*. Student must take time and think through each movement. Hands reach out first on *rabbit hop*. *Top* of head does *not* touch mat on roll.

Lesson 2   STATION ◁3▷ HOPPING AND JUMPING WITH BALL BOUNCING IN TIRES   17th Week

PERFORMANCE OBJECTIVES
   By hopping and jumping while bouncing ball in tire pattern, student demonstrates locomotor coordination, hand-eye coordination and space awareness.

(2)

EQUIPMENT
   Ball and 5 bike tires.

CHALLENGES
   1) Student carries ball in hands and hops on one foot through the tire pattern. (Hops are continuous on the same foot. *No* ball bouncing.)
   2) Student carries ball, hops on right foot into first tire, then bounces and catches ball in the 2nd tire without losing balance. This same sequence continues through each of the 5 tires. (Bounce and catch followed by a hop, etc.)
   3) Student performs same challenge as in 2) above hopping on *left* foot.
   4) If time allows, challenge student to *jump* into first tire and bounce ball into 2nd tire, but then jump into 3rd tire. This means the student does not jump into the tire where ball is bounced, but instead performs a *long* jump over this tire. The ball is bounced in the 2nd and 4th tires.

STRESS: Student holds ball over tire, and pushes it down into tire opening, not just dropping the ball. Student does *not* lean forward on hopping. Weight remains on one foot when hopping and 2 feet when jumping.

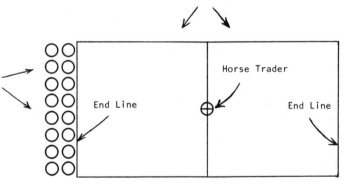

(1)

PERFORMANCE OBJECTIVES
   By vaulting over an intermediate board, student demonstrates tactile and kinesthetic stimulation, body
   awareness, and locomotor coordination.

EQUIPMENT
   Intermediate walking board and mats.

CHALLENGES
   1) Student grips intermediate walking board
      (one hand on each side) near center of board and vaults (lifts) legs over board,
      landing on opposite side. *Feet and legs are kept together* with knees bending
      before pushing off from feet. Student next vaults back to starting position.
   2) Student starts at one end of board, and continues to vault back
      and forth over the board until reaching the opposite end. (3 or
      4 vaults should move student from one end of board to the other.)

STRESS: Firm grip on board and strong push from toes with *high* lifting of knees to
        clear board with feet. Knees bend on take-off and landing. Hands do *not*
        release from board on the vault until feet arrive back on the floor.
        Use board at about the 12" intermediate height. (Students needing a
        greater challenge may wish to try vaulting over the 20" high board.)

Lesson 2   GAME - *ALL THE HORSES RUN*   17 & 18th Week

PERFORMANCE OBJECTIVES
   By performing in the *All The Horses
   Run* game, student demonstrates running and dodging, and tagging
   (with-out pushing) skills.

EQUIPMENT
   None.

DIRECTIONS
   1) To start the game, students line
      up behind one of 2 end lines with
      one student designated as the
      "Horse Trader" positioned in
      the center of the playing area
      midway between the 2 end lines.
   2) The "Horse Trader" calls out the name of one student whom he or she wants to challenge.
      This person attempts to run to the opposite end line (stable) without being tagged by the
      "Horse Trader". If he is tagged, he joins the "Horse Trader" in the center area.
   3) If the student called out to run succeeds in crossing the opposite end
      line, he yells out "All The Horses Run", and everyone starts running
      across the field to the opposite end line (the stables).
   4) The "Horse Trader" attempts to tag as many of these students (horses) as
      possible before they reach the safety of the opposite end line (stables).
   5) All students (horses) tagged join the Horse Trader in the center area
      and now serve as helpers in trying to tag other students.
   6) The game continues with the Horse Trader calling out one or more students to run
      back towards the starting line. The number of students (horses) called to run
      should generally equal the number of helpers the Horse Trader has captured (tagged).
   7) The Horse Trader is the only student who is permitted to call out names of
      students to run. He may at any time call out "All The Horses Run", but pre-
      ferably this should be done after he has captured many helpers.

8) The last student caught is the winner of the game, and if a new
   game is started, he or she becomes the "Horse Trader".

TEACHING SUGGESTIONS
1) For safety, it is best to play this game on a grassy area.
2) Emphasize that all helpers (taggers) must be at midline (center area) before anyone is
   called to run. No runners should begin running until all names have been called out.
3) Each time a runner makes it safely across the opposite
   end line, that is the signal for all the horses to run.
4) For variation the Horse Trader may call out "All The
   Boy Horses", or "All The Girl Horses Run".
5) Clothing colors may also be designated such as all the horses wearing blue or green, etc.

Lesson 1   MOVEMENT EXPLORATION WITH PARACHUTE   18th Week

PERFORMANCE OBJECTIVES
   By performing the following challenges, student demonstrates
   group teamwork and locomotor skills (running, jumping, etc.).

(1)

EQUIPMENT
   Classroom-size parachute.

TEACHING SUGGESTIONS
1) For good control over the parachute, students should be spaced evenly around the
   canopy using an overhand grip (palms down).
2) In order to secure a firmer grip on the
   parachute, it is advisable to have students roll the edge of the canopy 5 to
   10 rolls (depends on design and size
   of chute) towards the center.
3) On windy days, students will find the parachute difficult to use effectively.
4) In this particular parachute lesson problem solving
   prefaces have already been added to the challenges.

CHALLENGES
1) How would you make large waves using the parachute?
2) Gripping the chute with both hands palms down, can you raise
   and lower the chute while keeping your arms extended?
3) Can you cross your arms and pull back hard on the parachute while I count to 6?
4) Show me how you can raise the chute over your heads then release
   it, and quickly grab it again before it floats out of reach.
5) Try passing the parachute around in a circle without
   moving your feet. Move your hands quickly!
6) Let's try this challenge again, but if I blow the whistle, quickly change directions.
7) How fast can you roll the canopy towards the center
   with the chute kept tight at all times?
8) This time, keeping the parachute tight, see if you can
   squat down together and seal it against the ground.
9) Can you run in a circle holding the chute high over your heads with your right hands?
10) Now try this same task using your left hands.
11) Holding the parachute in your right hand, try hopping
    around in a circle by using your right foot.
12) This time, if I blow the whistle, you must change
    hands and change feet while hopping in a circle.
13) Let's hold the parachute in both hands keeping it tight and slide sideways to your right.
    If I blow the whistle, you must quickly change directions and slide to your left.
14) Show me how you can hold the parachute at a high level while running at a low level.

15) Can you inflate the parachute, jump 3 times
towards the center and then 3 jumps back out?
16) As a final challenge, show me how you can do something
new and different using the parachute.

Lesson 2   STATION ◁1▷ LOW AND HIGH WALKING BOARDS   18th Week

PERFORMANCE OBJECTIVES
By *cat walking* on a low board, and performing *heel-toe balance walk* with bean
bag on head on high board, student
demonstrates dynamic balance, laterality, and visual-motor coordination.

(1)

EQUIPMENT
Low and high walking boards, bean bag and mats.

CHALLENGES
1) *LOW BOARD* - Walk forward balancing on hands and
feet (*cat walk*) until reaching the end of the board.
2) *HIGH BOARD* - Walk forward balancing a bean bag on top of head and using a
heel-toe balance walk. (Heel of one foot is placed against toes of the other foot.)

STRESS: *LOW BOARD* - The hands lead the movement and stay out in front of the
body. Fingers must firmly grip the sides of the board. *HIGH BOARD* -
The heel of the back foot is placed against the toes of the front foot.

Lesson 2   STATION ◁2▷ JUMP BOX   18th Week

PERFORMANCE OBJECTIVES
By moving up coordination ladder, jumping
from jump box, and landing in tires, student demonstrates dynamic balance, space
awareness, tactile and kinesthetic stimulation, and foot-eye coordination.

(1)

EQUIPMENT
Jump box, coordination ladder,
3 bike tires and mats.

CHALLENGES
Ladder is attached to top of jump box.
It should fit firmly in place with end rung of ladder resting on top of box.
1) Walk forward on hands and feet (*4-legged walk*) using *rungs* of ladder
until reaching top of box. Jump from box into tire of choice.
2) Walk forward on *rungs* of ladder until reaching top of box. Jump
from box into tire of choice. (3 tires as targets.) Student
attempts to land with complete body control in selected tire.
3) Walk up ladder using either challenge (1) or (2) method, and
assume jumping position on top of box. Jump out from box, clap
hands above head, and land with good balance in tire of choice.

STRESS: Slow movements with emphasis on control of body. Bending
of knees on both the take-off and landing of each jump.

PERFORMANCE OBJECTIVES
  By hopping on a rebounder, student demonstrates unilateral control, body awareness, and dynamic balance.

EQUIPMENT
  Rebounder and mats.

CHALLENGES
  1) *REVIEW: JUMPING JACKS* - Student starts with
     feet together over center point of rebounder
     and arms down at sides. Student rebounds and
     performs a series of jumping jacks. Arms and
     legs move in a coordinated rhythmic sequence.
  2) *HOPPING* - Student starts with weight on one foot (preferred
     foot) over center point of rebounder and performs a series
     of 3-5 hops on this preferred foot maintaining controlled
     rhythmic movement. Student performs same hopping task on opposite foot.

(2)

STRESS: *HOPPING* - Head is up and shoulders back. Eyes look straight
          ahead. Arms help to maintain balance. Body position must be
          maintained on one foot over center point of rebounder.

PERFORMANCE OBJECTIVES
  By moving over a combination cross bar, tire
  and rope obstacle pattern in various ways,
  student demonstrates locomotor skill and
  coordination, dynamic balance, space
  awareness, and motor planning ability.

(3)

EQUIPMENT
  Two cross bars, 4 bike tires, and 3 jump ropes.

CHALLENGES
  1) Student jumps over cross bar and lands in first tire followed by a series of jumps
     back and forth over rope (with feet kept together) until reaching 2nd
     tire. Landing for each jump is made on opposite side of rope.
  2) Student performs a *heel-toe balance walk* moving forward on top of rope until reaching
     the 3rd tire. (Heel of one foot is placed against toes of other foot on each step.)
  3) Student performs a series of hops back and forth over rope until reaching
     the 4th tire. Hop may be accomplished on either the right or left foot.
  4) Movement pattern is completed with a hop from the 4th tire over
     the cross bar with a landing made on the take-off foot.

STRESS: Controlled movement, *not* speed. Good body alignment on all movements.
          Both feet leaving floor at same time on jump. Correct use of arms.

PERFORMANCE OBJECTIVES
  By performing the following challenges, student demonstrates *(One Bean Bag* 1)
  skill in throwing with partner and catching with partner.

EQUIPMENT
  Classroom set of bean bags.

TEACHING SUGGESTIONS

1) Participants should be paired with a partner. Each partner should have a bean bag in their possession. Some tasks will be attempted using only one bean bag while others will require *each* partner to have a bag.
2) Distance between partners will vary according to the skills to be practiced. Adequate spacing must be allowed between participants.

CHALLENGES

ONE BEAN BAG

1) Show me how you can toss and catch the bean bag with your partner.
2) Try using an underhand toss with one hand, but catch the bean bag by using 2 hands.
3) Can you toss and catch your bean bag using just one hand for both tossing and catching?
4) This time try tossing the bean bag up high back and forth to your partner.
5) Can you toss low with your partner, but each throw you must make your partner catch the bean bag closer to the ground? Start your first throw at waist level and work down.
6) Who can throw and catch with their partner by using different hands? You must throw with one hand and catch with the other.
7) Let's see if we can make our partner think. Just before throwing the bean bag to your partner, call out either "right", or "left", or "both". Your partner must catch the bean bag using the correct hand or hands. Use an underhand throw.

TWO BEAN BAGS

1) We are now going to try using 2 bean bags at the same time. Each partner should have their own bean bag. Show me how you would toss and catch the bean bags with your partner, but without having them collide. Both partners should throw at the same time.
2) How would you keep your body moving around in the available space, but still exchange the bean bags with your partner?
3) This time see if you can toss and catch the bean bags with your partner, but you must clap your hands before catching each bean bag.
4) For the next few challenges I would like you to stand back to back with your partner.
5) Show me how quickly you can pass the bean bags around your bodies by passing them from hand to hand. You must coordinate your hand movements with your partner!
6) This time, if I blow the whistle you must stop the bean bags, and then quickly change the passing direction.
7) Try passing just one bean bag around your bodies from hand to hand. You will find this more difficult than passing 2 bean bags.
8) As a final challenge you are going to play a game with your partner called *bean bag grab*. Sit down on the ground and place one bean bag between you and your partner. Your legs should be crossed with hands placed on your hips. I am going to call out either "right", "left", or "both". The first partner grabbing the bean bag with the correct hand or hands, and picking it up, will receive one point. If you grab it with the wrong hand, your partner gets the point. The first partner scoring 5 points wins the game.

Lesson 2   STATION ◁1▷ REBOUNDER   19th Week

(2)

PERFORMANCE OBJECTIVES

By performing alternate foot hopping pattern on a rebounder, student demonstrates unilateral control, body awareness, and dynamic balance.

EQUIPMENT

Rebounder and mats.

CHALLENGES

1) *REVIEW: HOPPING* - Student performs a series of 3-5 hops on preferred foot over center point of rebounder. If successful on preferred foot, student should be challenged to perform a series of 3-5 hops on the opposite foot.
2) *ALTERNATE HOPPING* - Student starts on preferred foot and hops 2 times, and without breaking rhythm changes to opposite foot and hops 2 times. This same rhythmic ("2-2" count) hopping pattern continues through a series of alternate hops.

STRESS: Head up and shoulders back with eyes looking straight ahead.
Arms help to maintain balance. Student attempts to maintain
controlled rhythmic movement on each side (foot) of the body.
Have student practice on floor before performing on rebounder.

Lesson 2   STATION ◁2▷ MAT STUNTS   19th Week

PERFORMANCE OBJECTIVES
By performing *modified push-ups*, and *wheelbarrow
walking*, student demonstrates upper body strength,
body awareness, and kinesthetic stimulation.

(1)

(2)

EQUIPMENT
Mats.

CHALLENGES
1) *MODIFIED PUSH-UP* - Student kneels and places hands flat on mat under shoulders with
arms extended straight and feet held off the mat. Body is straight from head to
knees in an inclined position. To perform the push-up the body is lowered until
chin or chest touches mat and then raised (pushed) back to starting position. Body
remains straight. Student attempts to do 6 to 12 push-ups in succession. (5 or 6
students can perform push-up at same time positioned across the mats.
You may wish to use verbal cues "down", "up", etc., for group response.)
2) *WHEELBARROW WALK* - Students work with partners. One student walks on hands while partner
supports (holds) legs between ankles and knees so that legs are straight and *off* the floor.
When reaching end of mats, partners change positions and return to starting position.

STRESS: *MODIFIED PUSH-UP* - Body is kept straight, feet off mat, and stomach area
does *not* touch mat when body is lowered. *WHEELBARROW WALK* - Arms are kept
straight and support body weight. Hands are flat on the mat.

Lesson 2   STATION ◁3▷ ANIMAL MOVEMENTS WITH TIRES   19th Week

PERFORMANCE OBJECTIVES
By moving through a tire pattern in various ways, student
demonstrates body and space awareness, laterality,
and motor planning ability.

(1)

EQUIPMENT
Eight bike tires.

CHALLENGES
1) Can you move through the tires like a kangaroo? (Jumping with arms crossed.)
2) Can you move through the tires like a 4-legged animal?
(Hands and feet placed in tire openings.)
3) How would a stork or one-legged animal move through the tires? (Student uses a hop.)
4) Show me a different way of traveling through the tires. (*Rabbit hop, crab walk*, etc.)

STRESS: Hands and feet are placed inside of tire openings. Student moves
only as fast as complete body control can be maintained. (Student
attempts to move through pattern without touching tires.)

Lesson 2   STATION ◁4▷ REBOUND NET AND LAUNCHING BOARD   19th Week

PERFORMANCE OBJECTIVES
By *reaction catching* with partner, and by catching 2 bean bags,
one in each hand from a launching board, student demonstrates
hand-eye coordination, laterality, and tactile awareness.

(2)

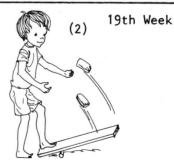

65

EQUIPMENT
Rebound net, launching board and classroom set of bean bags.

CHALLENGES
1) *REBOUND NET* - Student tosses bean bag against net, and partner concentrates on catching with fingers and hands. Students toss bag back and forth against net while alternating throwing and catching. Students see how long they can go without a miss.
2) *LAUNCHING BOARD* - Student steps on board and attempts to launch and catch 2 bags. Encourage student to attempt to catch one bag in each hand rather than both bags in hands cupped together. For students having success, use 2 different colored bags, and challenge student to catch a different color in each hand as you direct. Ocular pursuit training is enhanced when hand is directed individually to bag. Allow about 10 trials on each turn. Bags are placed side by side across end of board. (Those students lacking in skill and perceptual-motor ability necessary to be successful in catching 2 bags should stay with one bag only, or work on catching 2 bags using hands cupped together.)

STRESS: *REBOUND NET* - The eyes focus on the bag. Hands form catching pocket with fingers spread and move as a unit to bag. Accuracy and speed of throw is vital to successful catching. *LAUNCHING BOARD* - Hands work individually when attempting to catch 2 bags.

Lesson 3   GAME - *NORWEGIAN KICKBALL*   19th & 20th Week

PERFORMANCE OBJECTIVES
By performing in the *Norwegian Kickball* game, student demonstrates kicking a rolling ball, fielding and catching a kicked ball, passing ball with teamwork, and running around team.

EQUIPMENT
Kickball.

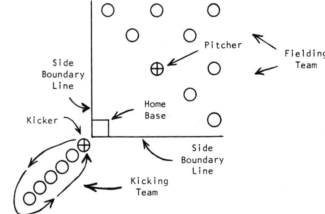

DIRECTIONS
1) Two equal teams of students are selected. (6 to 12 students on each team.)
2) One team is positioned in the field as shown while the other team is lined up behind home base in a straight line (single file) waiting their turn to kick.
3) The number one student on the "kicking" team stands just behind home base ready to kick the ball which is rolled (pitched) by the pitcher.
4) As soon as the ball is kicked, the kicker begins running around his own team as shown by the arrow in the diagram.
5) A student on the "fielding" team attempts to field or catch the kicked ball. Immediately all the students on the "fielding" team line up in single file formation behind the student who has the ball.
6) The ball is next passed from hand to hand over the heads of the students (single file formation) on the "fielding" team.
7) When the ball reaches the last student in line, he or she calls out "Stop".
8) If the runner (kicker) has *not* succeeded in encircling his team a designated number of times (usually 3-5 times), he is *out*; if he *has* succeeded, he scores a *run* for his team.
9) Three outs normally would retire the side and the teams change places, but the game may be varied by allowing the "kicking" team to remain as kickers until all students on the team have received their turn to kick.
10) *Foul* balls kicked outside of the side boundary lines do not count. Four foul balls makes the kicker out, but this rule is optional.

TEACHING SUGGESTIONS
1) When a large number of students are participating in the game, decrease the number of times the runner must encircle his team. When the teams are small, increase the number of times the runner must encircle his team. This is the "key" factor in keeping the game exciting and challenging.
2) If a team is not able to score, suggest that the students on the "kicking" team stand closer together.
3) An optional rule which adds to the game, is to require the "kicking" team to call out the number of times the runner has encircled the team each time he passes the front student.
4) The teacher may also require each student on the "fielding" team to be in line before the student with the ball begins passing it.

Lesson 1   MOVEMENT EXPLORATION WITH BALLS   20th Week

PERFORMANCE OBJECTIVES
By performing the following challenges, student demonstrates foot dribbling, trapping and volleying skills.

EQUIPMENT
Classroom set of rubber balls.

TEACHING SUGGESTIONS
1) Each participant should have a ball in his or her possession to begin the lesson.
2) A "scatter" formation within a designated area is used with each student standing in his or her own "personal" space. Enough space must be allowed between participants so that they can practice skills without interfering with each other's performance.
3) Use a whistle for control purposes.

CHALLENGES

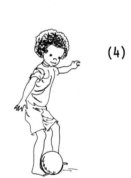
(4)

1) Show me how you can hold the ball between your feet.
2) Keeping the ball between your feet, can you walk around in a small circle without losing the ball?
3) Can you tap the ball back and forth between your feet without losing control? You are now beginning to dribble the ball.
4) Who can dribble the ball by using just the insides of their feet? Your toes should *not* touch the ball.
5) Try dribbling the ball around in a small circle by using either the inside or outside of both feet, but *not* your toes.
6) This time as you are dribbling your ball, show me how you would stop the ball by using just one foot.

HEEL TRAP - One of the best ways of stopping the ball with your feet is to trap it between the heel of one foot and the ground.
1) See if you can dribble the ball between the sides of your feet and then stop the ball by using a *heel trap.*
2) This time, try dribbling the ball as you move about your area, but always look for big spaces to move into. If I blow the whistle you must *heel trap* the ball. When the whistle blows again, continue to dribble the ball until the signal comes to trap it.
3) How many students can dribble their ball by using "quick" feet? This means you must move your feet quickly and control the ball by using the sides of your feet.
4) What other things can your feet do with the ball?

VOLLEY - The next group of challenges will focus on using fingers to volley (tap) the ball.
1) Using your hands, can you toss the ball up into the air and catch it above your head? Are your thumbs in close forming a pocket with your fingers spread?
2) Show me how you can perform this same skill, but catch the ball by using your finger tips with your elbows pointing out towards the sides of your body.
3) Try tossing the ball up over your head, tap the ball once with your finger tips and then catch it. This is called *volleying* the ball.
4) Who can toss the ball up over their head, *volley* (tap) it *high* with their finger tips and then catch it?

67

5) How many of you can *volley* the ball 2 times in a row before catching it?
6) As a final challenge, see how many times you can *volley* the ball in succession before catching it. Remember to keep your fingers in close as you *volley* the ball!

Lesson 2　　　　　　STATION ◁1▷ LOW AND HIGH WALKING BOARDS　　　　20th Week

PERFORMANCE OBJECTIVES
　By dribbling ball in hoops along low board, and by balancing tires on each wrist on high board, student demonstrates dynamic balance, hand-eye coordination, laterality, and tactile stimulation.

EQUIPMENT
　Low and high walking boards, rubber ball, 2 hoops, 2 bike tires and mats.

CHALLENGES
　1) *LOW BOARD* – Walk forward, carrying rubber ball, dribble ball 5 times in hoop placed on left side of board, then dribble ball 5 times in hoop placed on right side of board. (Students lacking in hand-eye coordination skill needed for dribbling the ball may use a modified bounce and catch.)
　2) *HIGH BOARD* – Walk forward to center of board while balancing a bicycle tire on each wrist, make a ½ turn at center of board, and walk backward to the end of the board.

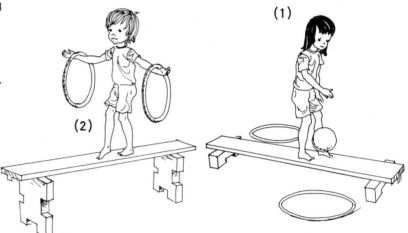

(1)

(2)

STRESS: *LOW BOARD* – When dribbling the ball, the left hand is used on the left side of the board and the right hand is used on the right side of the board. Finger tips push the ball down on the dribble, not slapping. *HIGH BOARD* – Arms are held out at shoulder level while balancing tires on each wrist. Head is held erect.

Lesson 2　　　　　　STATION ◁2▷ JUMP BOX OBSTACLE COURSE　　　　20th Week

PERFORMANCE OBJECTIVES
　By moving up a coordination ladder, jumping from a jump box, and moving through a tire and cross bar pattern, student demonstrates locomotor coordination, dynamic balance, body and space awareness, directionality, and motor planning ability.

(4)

EQUIPMENT
　Coordination ladder, jump box, red bike tire, 2 cross bars and mats.

CHALLENGES
　Ladder is attached to top of jump box. It should fit firmly in place with end rung of ladder resting on top of box.
　1) Student *dog walks* (on hands and feet) up inclined ladder to top of jump box.
　　(May also challenge student to move up ladder using other body movements.)
　2) Student jumps from box into red tire target which is placed close to cross bar on mats.
　3) Student performs *forward roll* over low cross bar without touching bar. (Hands are placed on mat on opposite side of cross bar.)
　4) Student crawls under low cross bar without touching bar.

STRESS: Landing on "soft" part of feet (not flat-footed) with low bending of knees for good body control and balance. On the *forward roll*, the hands are placed over the cross bar on opposite side and close to the bar. The hips lead the body over on the roll with the head coming under the body in a tucked position. The *top* of the head does *not* touch the mat, only the back of the head.

Lesson 2   STATION ◁3▷ REBOUNDER   20th Week

PERFORMANCE OBJECTIVES
   By performing combination hops and jumps while rebounding on a rebounder, student demonstrates laterality, body awareness, motor planning ability, and dynamic balance.

EQUIPMENT
   Rebounder and mats.

CHALLENGES
   1) *REVIEW: ALTERNATE HOPPING* – Student starts on preferred foot and hops 2 times. Without breaking rhythm and losing control, student changes to opposite foot and hops 2 times. Student continues this same rhythmic pattern ("2-2" count) through a series of alternate foot hopping.
   2) *COMBINATION HOPS AND JUMPS* – Student performs a coordinated sequence of hopping and jumping movements by rebounding on the right foot twice, left foot twice, and then both feet twice. This same coordinated sequence is repeated through a continuous series of movements.

STRESS: Good body posture with head up and shoulders back. Eyes look straight ahead and *not* down at feet. *COMBINATION HOPS AND JUMPS* – Weight is controlled over one foot when hopping, and 2 feet when jumping.

Lesson 2   STATION ◁4▷ TIRE AND ROPE MAZE   20th Week

PERFORMANCE OBJECTIVES
   By moving through tire and rope pattern in various ways, student demonstrates locomotor coordination, balance, space awareness, directionality, and motor planning ability.

EQUIPMENT
   Two long ropes, 4 short jump ropes, and 5 bike tires.

CHALLENGES
   1) Challenge student to jump through maze using a jump, *straddle jump*, jump, *straddle jump*, etc., motor pattern. First jump is into tire 1, followed by a *straddle jump* with feet landing outside of parallel side ropes. Next jump is into tire 2 followed by a *straddle jump*, etc.
   2) Challenge student to jump through tires by moving *sideways* with right side leading, then through again with left side leading.
   3) Challenge student to hop through the maze on one foot moving forward and through again moving sideways.
   4) Challenge student to find a different way of moving through the maze.

STRESS: Controlled movements, *not* speed! Student attempts *not* to touch tires or ropes while moving through the maze.

69

MOVEMENT EXPLORATION WITH RHYTHM STICKS

(1)

PERFORMANCE OBJECTIVES
By performing the following challenges, student demonstrates bilateral (2 hands) finger dexterity, and bilateral (2 hands) hand-eye coordination.

EQUIPMENT
Classroom set of rhythm sticks.

TEACHING SUGGESTIONS
1) Each participant should have *two* rhythm sticks in his or her possession to begin the lesson (one stick in each hand). If enough sticks are not available for each student to have 2, then some students can work with only one stick.
2) Adequate spacing is important along with a definite signal which participants understand means to stop activity and listen.

CHALLENGES
1) Holding one stick in each hand, show me how you can make your fingers crawl up and down the trees (sticks).
2) Can you hold one stick in each hand (horizontally) and make your fingers roll it forward and then backwards like riding on top of a log?
3) Who can twirl their sticks in and out of their fingers like twirling a baton? Both sticks must be moving at the same time.
4) Using one stick as a hammer and the other stick as a long nail, see if you can hammer the nail down through a hole formed by cupping one hand around the bottom of the nail.
5) Now try it again by using opposite hands.
6) How many of you can do it with your eyes closed? (Tactile and kinesthetic senses stressed here.)
7) Try holding both sticks in front of your body (horizontally) like 2 poles lying on their side and see if you can punch the poles (hit ends together) through your hands.
8) Close your eyes and try punching the poles through your hands.
9) Place both sticks on the ground in front of your body and take a kneeling position. On signal to begin, pick up one stick and begin passing it around your body (hand to hand, and then set it back down in front of your body. Now do the same movement with the other stick. Can you go fast and do it again?
10) This time when I blow the whistle, see if you can quickly change directions of the movement.
11) Show me how you can pass the sticks around your body with your eyes closed.
12) Holding a stick in each hand, can you flip them over one time only, and catch one stick in each hand? This is called *flip the pancake over*.
13) Who can toss their sticks from hand to hand like a juggler?
14) How would you make the letter "T" with your sticks? Can you balance one stick on the ground, and then balance the other stick across the top of it?
15) Who can jump back and forth over the top of the "T" without knocking it over?
16) As a final challenge, I am going to *tap* out a variety of sound patterns by using both sticks at the same time or by alternating sticks. After tapping out each sound pattern, I will raise my sticks up over my head. This will be your signal to repeat the same sound pattern with your own sticks.

Lesson 2   STATION ◁1▷ REBOUNDER   21st Week

PERFORMANCE OBJECTIVES
By rebounding on a rebounder and catching a thrown ball, student demonstrates dynamic balance, body awareness, and hand-eye coordination.

EQUIPMENT
Rebounder, ball, and mats.

(2)

CHALLENGES
1) *REVIEW: COMBINATION HOPS AND JUMPS* - Student performs coordin-

ated sequence of hopping and jumping by rebounding twice on:
right foot, left foot, and both feet. Repeat in a series.
2) *REBOUNDING WITH BALL CATCHING* - Student rebounds and catches
ball thrown underhand by teacher. Student tosses ball back
to teacher while maintaining rhythmic rebounding. Student
rebounds while catching and tossing ball 3-5 times.

STRESS: *REBOUNDING WITH BALL CATCHING* - Eyes watch ball into hands on
   catch. Hands must prepare to receive ball. Student must stay
   over rebounder center. Student makes catch in the air. Proper
   timing on ball toss by teacher is important for successful performance.

Lesson 2   STATION ◇2◇ MAT STUNT   21st Week

PERFORMANCE OBJECTIVES
   By performing *timber fall*, and
   knee walk, student demonstrates
   balance, body awareness,
   and kinesthesis.

EQUIPMENT
   Mats.

CHALLENGES
   1) *TIMBER FALL* - Participants kneel alongside of mat with arms and hands against sides of
   body. Body is straight from head to knees. On verbal cue of "timber", they fall forward
   from knee position to a prone position. As body falls forward, the arms extend out and
   forward with the hands striking the mat first to break the fall. The head is turned
   sideways before contacting the mat. Have the participants try the stunt several times.
   2) *KNEE WALK* - Student kneels on one end of mat, and then lifts feet from
   mat and maintains balance on *knees only*. Student walks to opposite end
   of mats attempting to maintain balanced position on knees. Body is kept
   straight from head to knees. Teacher can make stunt more difficult by
   requiring student to reach back and hold ankles while walking on knees.

STRESS: *TIMBER FALL* - Hands break fall. Participants respond as a group.
   KNEE WALK - Head and shoulders are back, not leaning forward.

Lesson 2   STATION ◇3◇ BALL DRIBBLING THROUGH HOOP PATTERN   21st Week

PERFORMANCE OBJECTIVES
   By dribbling a ball through a hoop pattern,
   student demonstrates hand-eye coordination,
   space awareness, and tactile stimulation.

EQUIPMENT
   Ball and 4 hoops.

CHALLENGES
   1) Student attempts to dribble a rubber
   ball through the hoop pattern without touching the hoops and without losing control of the ball.
   2) Student attempts to dribble the ball a definite number of times in each hoop as challenged
   by the instructor. (Students unable to experience success using a dribble
   may have to modify task to a combination dribble and bounce-catch.)

STRESS: Using a push on the dribble with "soft" fingers and *not* a slapping
   motion. Fingers are spread and stay close to ball. Student attempts
   to move through hoops without stopping the dribble.

71

Lesson 2   STATION ◁4▷ SCOOTER BOARD   21st Week

PERFORMANCE OBJECTIVES
   By moving on a scooter board around an obstacle, student demonstrates laterality, body
   awareness, upper body strength, and kinesthesis.   (1)

EQUIPMENT
   Scooter board and traffic cone.

CHALLENGES
   1) Student walks on hands with legs extended and feet resting on scooter board, and
      attempts to travel around traffic cone without touching
      cone. (Similar to *seal walk*.)
   2) Student sits on scooter board and moves around traffic cone using the feet only (no hands).

STRESS: In challenge (1), body kept straight with elbows stiff and
        feet must press down on scooter board to maintain control.

Lesson 3   GAME - *WHISTLE MIXER*   21st & 22nd Week

PERFORMANCE OBJECTIVES
   By performing in the *Whistle Mixer* game, student
   demonstrates listening skills, and locomotor skills.

EQUIPMENT
   Whistle.

DIRECTIONS
   1) Students are scattered throughout the playing area.
   2) To begin the game, students walk around in any direction they wish but cannot touch.
      (They may also be challenged to skip, run, hop, or jump, etc.)
   3) The teacher blows the whistle a specific number of times
      in succession with short, sharp blasts.
   4) The students must respond according to the number of whistle blasts and
      form small circles with the number of students forming the circle equal
      to the number of times the whistle is blown. (Example: If the whistle
      is blown 4 times, the students form a circle of 4 students, *no more, no less*.)
   5) Any student left out (not forming in a circle) is eliminated. Also, if a circle is
      formed with more than the specified number of students, the entire circle is eliminated.
   6) Eliminated students become game judges or officials on the sideline of the playing area.
   7) The teacher now gives a new movement challenge and the game contin-
      ues with students moving individually in different directions.
   8) The game can continue until just 2 students are left who are declared the winners.

TEACHING SUGGESTIONS
   1) If played inside (multi-purpose room) music can be added to make the game more enjoyable.
   2) A good variation is to modify the elimination rule so that students are only
      eliminated for one turn. This keeps most students active at all times.

Lesson 1   MOVEMENT EXPLORATION WITH ROPES   22nd Week

PERFORMANCE OBJECTIVES
   By performing the following challenges, student
   demonstrates rope jumping, and rope hopping.

EQUIPMENT
   Classroom set of jump ropes.

(7)

TEACHING SUGGESTIONS
  1) Each student should have a rope in his or her possession to begin the lesson.
  2) Establish a system of distributing and collecting the ropes.
  3) Adequate space for movement must be allowed between participants.
  4) Stress that students listen to the entire challenge before starting to move.

CHALLENGES
  1) Holding both ends of your rope just in front of your feet, show me how you can jump
     back and forth over the rope without moving it. Try keeping your feet together!
  2) This time hold your rope in the same position and see if you
     can hop back and forth over the rope by using your left foot.
  3) Try repeating this same challenge, only this time use your *right* foot.
  4) Who can make their rope swing slowly back and forth under their feet, and
     jump it with both feet held together? Jump forwards and backwards.
  5) How many students can hold their rope several feet in front of their body, then
     drag the rope towards their feet and jump it just before it reaches their toes?
  6) Show me how you can turn the rope over your head, then drag it
     toward your feet and jump it just before it reaches your toes.
  7) This time, try turning your rope faster and jump it one
     time just before reaching your toes.
  8) Who can jump their rope 2 times in succession without hitting
     the rope with their feet? 3 times? 4 times? (etc.)
  9) Carefully count your jumps and see how many times
     you can turn your rope and jump it without a miss.
 10) How many of you can turn your rope and hop over it on just one foot?
 11) Try this same challenge by using your other foot.
 12) Who can change feet while hopping over their rope? Left foot, then right foot, etc.
 13) Show me how you would hop over your rope 2 times
     on the left foot, then 2 times on the right foot.
 14) Are there any students who think they can jump over
     their rope with their eyes closed? Let's all try it!
 15) Can anyone jump their rope 10 times in a row without looking?
 16) This time see if you can turn your rope backwards and jump over it.
 17) How many students can turn in a circle while jumping their rope?
 18) As a final challenge, I would like to see if you can do cross-overs?
     This is done by crossing your arms in an X as the rope comes over
     your head, then holding the X position until the rope passes under
     your feet. Your arms uncross as the rope passes over your head again.

Lesson 2   STATION ◁1▷ LOW AND HIGH WALKING BOARDS   22nd Week

PERFORMANCE OBJECTIVES
  By passing partner on low board, and by walking and watching swinging ball on high
  board, student demonstrates dynamic balance, ocular pursuit and position
  in space.

EQUIPMENT
  Ball, low and high walking board, small
  ball suspended by a cord and mats.

CHALLENGES
  1) *LOW BOARD* – One student starts at each end of walking
     board and slowly they walk toward each other. They
     attempt to pass in the middle of the board without
     stepping off the board and then continue walking for-
     ward to the end of the board. (A variation

and more difficult challenge is to have the partners tossing and
catching a ball as they walk toward each other.)
2) *HIGH BOARD* – Walk forward with eyes tracking (following) a swinging ball held by instructor at opposite end of board. Ball is held at eye level. (Use styrofoam or
plastic ball suspended by cord. If ball is not available use a bean bag tied to rope.)

STRESS: *HIGH BOARD* – Head does *not* move from side to side when tracking ball.
The eyes should follow the movement of the ball without head movement.

Lesson 2   STATION ◇2◇ COORDINATION LADDER   22nd Week

PERFORMANCE OBJECTIVES
By moving along a coordination ladder in
various ways, student demonstrates body
and space awareness, gross-motor coordination, hand-eye and foot-eye coordination.

(2)

EQUIPMENT
Coordination ladder, ball, and mats.

CHALLENGES
1) Can you walk on the rungs of the ladder while tossing and catching a rubber ball?
2) Show me how you would walk the ladder moving like a crab. (*crab walk*)
3) Who can travel on the rungs or sides of the ladder
   moving like a lame dog? (2 hands, and one leg.)
4) Find a way of moving from one end of the ladder to the
   other end that you have never used before.
5) (Use other verbal challenges requiring various types of
   thought processing and coordinated movements.)

STRESS: Listening skills and getting into a good starting position before moving on
         ladder. Hands in challenge (1) form pocket to catch ball using "soft fingers".

Lesson 2   STATION ◇3◇ JUMP BOX   22nd Week

PERFORMANCE OBJECTIVES
By performing a *scissors jump, heel click,*
and *ball grab jump* from jump box, student
demonstrates dynamic balance, awareness of
body and position in space, and kinesthesis.

(3)

EQUIPMENT
Jump box with incline
board, ball and mats.

CHALLENGES
1) *SCISSORS JUMP* – Student walks
   (or runs) up incline board,
   jumps from box and performs a *scissors jump*. On jump the student extends one leg
   forward and the other backwards in a scissors position. Landing
   is made with feet (together) in normal landing position.
2) *HEEL CLICK JUMP* – Student walks (or runs) up incline board, jumps from box, and
   clicks heels together. Landing is made in normal position with bent knees.
3) *BALL GRAB JUMP* – Student *walks* up incline board and takes correct jumping position
   on box. Student jumps from box and grabs a rubber ball held up high in front of
   box by instructor. (Ball is held in one hand extended out in front of jumper.
   Student grabs the ball held *stationary* by the instructor and lands with
   the ball clutched in both hands. Ball must be held at a level and distance where student must jump out and up to reach the ball.)

4) For students needing a greater challenge, add a *forward roll* while attempting to keep ball between knees.

STRESS: Student attempts to land with bent knees and complete body balance.

Lesson 2   STATION ◇4◇ REBOUNDER   22nd Week

PERFORMANCE OBJECTIVES
By throwing bean bag against net and catching it while rebounding on rebounder, student demonstrates visual-motor integration, bilateral coordination, and dynamic balance.

EQUIPMENT
Rebounder, bean bags, rebound net, ball, and mats.

CHALLENGES
1) *REVIEW: REBOUNDING WITH BALL CATCHING* - Student rebounds, catches ball thrown underhand by teacher, then tosses ball back while maintaining control. Repeat several times.
2) *REBOUNDING WITH BEAN BAG THROW AGAINST NET* - Student rebounds over rebounder center, and throws and catches bag bouncing off net. Net is on floor nearby. Task requires rebound and bag toss synchronization.

STRESS: *REBOUNDING WITH BEAN BAG THROW AGAINST NET* - Eyes visually follow bag from net to hands. Student must *not* lean so forward that balance is lost. Bean bag is thrown overhand. Place net for best return of bag. *FOR SAFETY* - Use "spotters".

Lesson 1   MOVEMENT EXPLORATION WITH HOOPS   23rd Week

PERFORMANCE OBJECTIVES
By performing the following challenges, student demonstrates jumping and hopping skills.

EQUIPMENT
Classroom set of hoops.

TEACHING SUGGESTIONS
1) Set up 5 hoop "patterns" on the playground as shown and then divide students up evenly into 5 groups. One group is assigned to begin at each of the 5 hoop "patterns". Each group of students performs at their assigned hoop "pattern" (or station) until the signal is given to rotate as a group to a new pattern.
2) A directed movement problem should be assigned for each hoop "pattern" as indicated.
3) Students should also be given the opportunity to explore and create their own sequence of movement after practicing the directed movement problem for several repetitions.

CHALLENGES
PATTERN 1
1) Hop through the hoops on your left foot.
2) Hop through the hoops on your right foot.

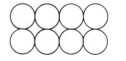
(1)

PATTERN 2
1) Run through the hoops.
2) *Straddle jump* (feet and legs spread apart) through the hoops.

(2)

PATTERN 3
1) Hop through the hoops by changing from your left foot, to your right foot, and back to your left foot according to where the hoops are placed.

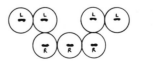
(3)

75

PATTERN 4
  1) Use a jump, *straddle jump*, jump, *straddle jump*, jump, jump.

(4)

PATTERN 5
  1) Jump through the hoops with your feet together.
  2) Jump through the hoops sideways.

(5)

Lesson 2   STATION <1> REBOUNDER   23rd Week

PERFORMANCE OBJECTIVES
  By rebounding on a rebounder with a bean bag balanced
  on top of head, student demonstrates object and dynamic balance, tactile awareness, and body control.

EQUIPMENT
  Rebounder, bean bags, rebound net, and mats.

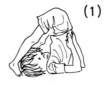

(2)

CHALLENGES
  1) *REVIEW: REBOUNDING WITH BEAN BAG THROW AGAINST NET* -
     Student rebounds over center area of rebounder while
     throwing and catching a bean bag against a rebound
     net. Net is set up on floor near the rebounder.
  2) *REBOUNDING WITH BEAN BAG ON HEAD* - Student
     places bean bag on top of head and is chal-
     lenged to rebound without the bean bag fall-
     ing off head. Student performs as many re-
     bounds as possible without bean bag falling from head.

STRESS: Good posture with body straight, shoulders back, head
        up. *REBOUNDING WITH BEAN BAG ON HEAD* - Light, low re-
        bounding which helps to maintain control of bean bag.

Lesson 2   STATION <2> MAT STUNTS   23rd Week

PERFORMANCE OBJECTIVES
  By *snail balancing* and *bicycle standing*,
  student demonstrates static balance, flexibility, body awareness, and kinesthesis.

(1)

(2)

EQUIPMENT
  Mats.

CHALLENGES
  1) *SNAIL BALANCE* - Student sits on mat and rolls back onto shoulders.
     Hands immediately are placed against back to support body as shown. Upper arms and
     elbows are braced against the mat. Legs are extended back across the head with the
     feet reaching for the mat. Student attempts to hold the snail position with toes
     touching the mat. Several students can perform this stunt
     at the same time, positioned across the mats.
  2) *BICYCLE STAND* - Starting position is the same for the *snail balance*. Student sits on mat
     and rolls back onto shoulders. Hands immediately are placed against the back for sup-
     porting the body. Upper arms and elbows are braced against the mat. Legs are extended

straight up with toes pointed. After securing and holding balance on shoulders, student attempts to pump the legs up and down as in pedalling a bicycle (see illustration).

STRESS: Hands must be placed against back (near the hips) to properly support body.
Spread fingers for firmer support. On the bicycle movement, the legs
are pumped up and down rather than waved back and forth.

Lesson 2   STATION ⟨3⟩ OBSTACLE COURSE   23rd Week

PERFORMANCE OBJECTIVES
By jumping and hopping through combinations
of tire and cross bar obstacles, student
demonstrates locomotor control, foot-
eye coordination, space awareness,
and motor planning ability.

EQUIPMENT
Ball, 3 cross bars, and
10 bike tires.

CHALLENGES
1) *PATTERN 1* - a) Student jumps through
   pattern as shown and performs a *straddle jump*
   into the 2 tires placed side by side (one foot into each
   tire);   b) Student jumps through pattern with feet kept
   together; c) Student jumps through pattern moving sideways.
2) *PATTERN 2* - a) Student jumps through pattern while holding *rubber ball between knees;*
   b) Student hops pattern on right foot only; c) Student hops pattern on left foot only.

STRESS: Bending of knees on take-off and landing. *No* flat-footed landings. Arms help to
lift body. (Raise cross bar according to skill level of individual participants.)

Lesson 2   STATION ⟨4⟩ REBOUND NET AND LAUNCHING BOARD   23rd Week

PERFORMANCE OBJECTIVES
By throwing and catching a rubber ball from a rebound net, and by launching and catching a rubber
ball from a launching board, student demonstrates
hand-eye coordination and tactile stimulation.

EQUIPMENT
Rebound net, launching board,
and 2 or more rubber balls.

CHALLENGES
1) *REBOUND NET* - Student passes (throws) a rubber
   ball against the net using a 2-handed chest
   pass, and catches the ball. The catch is made
   with fingers pointing up and forming a pocket
   for the ball. Allow 10 trials per turn for each participant.
2) *LAUNCHING BOARD* - Student steps on board and launches a rubber ball. Student
   attempts to clap hands before catching ball. Allow 5 to 10 trials on each turn.

STRESS: For extra motivation, have student keep count of his or her score allowing one
point for each successful catch on both the rebound net and launching board.
REBOUND NET - On chest pass, the finger tips conttol the ball. Student should
be encouraged to step towards the net before releasing the ball.

77

PERFORMANCE OBJECTIVES
   By performing in the *Hunters And Rabbits* game, student demonstrates basic locomotor movements, dodging, and throwing at a moving target.

EQUIPMENT
   Two balls.

DIRECTIONS
   1) To start the game, 2 students are designated as "Hunters" and each hunter is given a ball. The hunters position themselves in the center of the playing area.
   2) The remaining students are designated as "Rabbits", and they line up along one end line.
   3) The 2 hunters decide on a "movement challenge" for the rabbits and call it out. (Examples: run, hop, jump, walk, skip, etc.) All rabbits must move using the challenged movement.
   4) The 2 hunters must also perform the movement called out, and they attempt to touch or hit the rabbits with the ball before they make it safely to the *opposite* end line.
   5) The hunters may elect to touch the rabbits while holding the ball in their hands, or hit them by throwing the ball. A thrown ball, however, must hit a rabbit below waist level to count.
   6) If a student (rabbit) refuses to leave the safety of the end line, the hunters may count to 5 and then tag the student behind the end line.
   7) Hunters must have a ball in their possession in order to tag a rabbit which means that if a ball is thrown, they must retrieve it before they can tag another rabbit.
   8) The rabbits that are hit must remain stationary in the playing area where hit and they become "poison trees". A poison tree may reach out with its branches (arms and hands) and tag other rabbits who come near the tree. Any rabbit tagged in this manner also becomes a poison tree.
   9) Students (rabbits) moving outside the side boundary lines to avoid being hit or tagged are automatically caught at that spot and become poison trees.
  10) Each time the rabbits make it safely to the opposite end line, a new movement challenge is called out by the hunters.
  11) The last 2 rabbits caught are declared the game winners and they become the new hunters for the next game.

TEACHING SUGGESTIONS
   1) Do *not* allow the "poison trees" to move from the spot where caught in order to tag other rabbits.
   2) Hunters should be allowed to run after a thrown ball in order to retrieve it. However, once they arrive back at the boundary line of the playing area, they must move in the designated manner as called out.
   3) Hunters should be required to position themselves in the middle of the playing area until after making their movement challenge.
   4) This is a fun and exciting game for students, but adequate space must be allowed for the safety and enjoyment of all.

Lesson 1   MOVEMENT EXPLORATION WITH PARACHUTE   24th Week

PERFORMANCE OBJECTIVES
   By performing the following challenges, student demonstrates group teamwork, and inflation of parachute.

EQUIPMENT
Classroom parachute, 4 balls and bean bag.

TEACHING SUGGESTIONS
1) In this lesson a game approach will be used with
   2 teams competing against each other. The class
   is divided into 2 equal teams with one team
   spaced evenly on each half of the parachute.
2) Students should use a firm
   overhand grip (palms down).
3) On windy days the parachute is
   difficult to use outdoors.
4) Group teamwork must be
   stressed at all times.
5) The rules for each game introduced must be
   carefully explained before play begins.

(1)

CHALLENGES
Three game activities are suggested. Two or 3 game activities can be easily introduced in
one teaching period. Changing the games at frequent intervals provides more variety and
enthusiasm within any given lesson period. In order for games (2) and (3) listed below to
be successful, the students must be able to consistently get a good inflation on the parachute. Number should be called slightly before parachute reaches highest point of inflation.

1) *BALL BOUNCE* - A number of light balls (3 or 4) are placed on top of the parachute.
   On a signal to begin, each team attempts to shake the balls off on the other team's
   side of the chute. Balls are bounced off the parachute up into the air. Participants may not use their hands to keep the balls from leaving the chute. One point
   is awarded a team each time a ball leaves the parachute and touches the ground
   on their opponent's side. This game is also called *Ball Shake*.

2) *NUMBERS EXCHANGE* - Players on each team are given a number. (Each team should have
   players with corresponding numbers.) The chute is inflated and as it reaches the
   maximum height, a number is called out. The player on each team whose number is
   called must quickly run under the parachute and exchange places. The first player
   successfully reaching the opponent's place without having the chute touch the body
   scores one point for their team. Players can keep these places, and the game continues with a new number called out. If teachers desire not to have team competition, the game can be played as noted, but without awarding team points.

3) *STEAL THE BACON* - A bean bag or other small object is placed under the chute at
   approximately the center point. Players on each team are given a number. The
   students inflate the parachute and when it reaches its highest point, the teacher
   calls out a number. The player with that number from each team runs out and attempts to
   grab the bean bag and get back to his or her position without being tagged
   by their opponent. A player who successfully gets back to his or her team position
   without being tagged, or touched by the descending chute scores one point for
   his or her team.

Lesson 2   STATION <1> LOW AND HIGH WALKING BOARDS   (1)   24th Week

PERFORMANCE OBJECTIVES
By walking with closed eyes on low board,
and by tossing and catching ball on high
board, student demonstrates tactile
and kinesthetic awareness, dynamic
balance, and hand-eye coordination.

79

EQUIPMENT
  Low and high walking boards, blindfold, rubber ball, and mats.

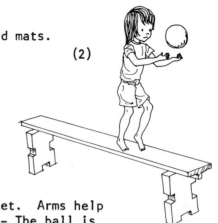
(2)

CHALLENGES
  1) *LOW BOARD* - Student walks forward slowly with
     eyes covered (or closed), and maintains balance
     on board. (Teacher or aide should walk along-
     side of student and offer help, if needed.
  2) *HIGH BOARD* - Student attempts to toss
     and catch a 7" rubber ball while
     walking slowly forward on board.

STRESS: *LOW BOARD* - Student carefully feels board with feet. Arms help
        to make adjustment in balance point. *HIGH BOARD* - The ball is
        tossed up after every 2 or 3 steps. Eyes watch ball into hands!

Lesson 2   STATION ⟨2⟩ JUMP BOX WITH COORDINATION LADDER   24th Week

PERFORMANCE OBJECTIVES
  By moving in various ways up and down a
  coordination ladder and incline board
  on jump box, student demonstrates gross-
  motor coordination, dynamic balance, body
  and space awareness, and kinesthesis.

(4)

EQUIPMENT
  Jump box with incline board,
  coordination ladder and mats.

CHALLENGES
  1) Student performs a *balance walk* on rungs of ladder until
     reaching top of box and then walks down incline board.
  2) Student performs a 4-legged *dog walk* on sides or rungs of ladder until reach-
     ing top of box, and then moves down incline board using a 4-legged walk.
  3) Student walks up incline board and then walks down
     ladder using a *balance walk* on rungs of ladder.
  4) Student walks up incline board using a 4-legged
     walk and then moves down ladder in same way.
  5) If time allows, have student creep up incline board on hands
     and knees and then perform a *crab walk* down the ladder.

STRESS: Slow controlled movements. Eyes carefully guide all movements.

Lesson 2   STATION ⟨3⟩ SCOOTER BOARD WITH OBSTACLES   24th Week

PERFORMANCE OBJECTIVES
  By performing a *partner wheelbarrow walk* around
  obstacles, student demonstrates upper arm
  strength, body awareness, and kinesthesis.

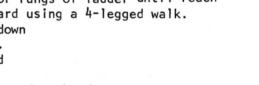
(1)

EQUIPMENT
  Scooter board, 2 traffic cones, and bean bag.

CHALLENGES
  1) *PARTNER WHEELBARROW WALK* - One partner
     assumes push-up position with hands gripping sides of scooter board. The 2nd partner
     grasps the first partner's legs, half way between the ankles and the knees. This
     person pushes and guides the wheelbarrow around the obstacles.
     On their next turn the partners change places.

2) *SCOOTER SWIM* - If time allows, have each student assume prone position on scooter board, and travel around obstacles using swim type arm movements. To make this task more challenging, ask the student to hold a bean bag between the feet without dropping it.

STRESS: *PARTNER WHEELBARROW WALK* - Pusher should be cautioned not to move too
        fast. Student may adjust hands to top of scooter board, if necessary.

Lesson 2   STATION ◇4◇ REBOUNDER   24th Week

PERFORMANCE OBJECTIVES
    By rebounding on a rebounder in synchronization with turning rope, student
    demonstrates locomotor control, rhythmic coordination, and dynamic balance.

EQUIPMENT
    Rebounder, jump rope, bean bag, and mats.

CHALLENGES
    1) *REVIEW: REBOUNDING WITH BEAN BAG ON HEAD* - Student
       rebounds with bean bag balanced on top of head.
       Student performs as many rebounds as possible
       without the bean bag falling from head.
    2) *REBOUNDING WITH ROPE TURNING* - Student rebounds
       over center area of rebounder while rhythmically
       turning a rope on side of body. Both ends of
       rope are held in one hand which turns the rope
       with same action as in rope jumping.

(2)

STRESS: Correct body alignment (not leaning forward)
        with controlled rebounding. *REBOUNDING WITH
        ROPE TURNING* - Feet rebound from surface of
        rebounder as turning rope strikes the surface.
        Wrist action controls the movement of the
        rope with arm remaining close to side of body.

Lesson 1   MOVEMENT EXPLORATION WITH BALLS   25th Week

PERFORMANCE OBJECTIVES
    By performing the following challenges, student demonstrates
    individual ball handling and partner ball handling skills.

EQUIPMENT
    Classroom set of rubber balls.

TEACHING SUGGESTIONS
    1) This lesson will review skills explored previously, but the verbal challenges will be
       different and the tasks a little more difficult. A creative approach will be used.
    2) For individual challenges, each participant should have a ball in his or her possession.
    3) Partner tasks will only require one ball for 2 participants.
    4) Do not allow silliness! Mental concentration is important
       to successful participation and learning.
    5) Adequate space must be allowed between participants so
       that skills can be practiced without interference.

(10)

CHALLENGES
    1) How many ways can you make the ball move around your body?
    2) Can you roll the ball around your stomach and back by using
       your fingers? When you hear the whistle, change directions.

3) Holding the ball out in front of your body, can you perform a ½ turn each time you hear the whistle?
4) How many different ways can you throw the ball to yourself?
5) Starting from a kneeling position, who can toss the ball up high, get to their feet and catch it?
6) Can anyone toss his or her ball up, then turn around one complete turn and catch it before it hits the ground? (This is a difficult challenge.)
7) What can you do with the ball by using only one hand?
8) Who can dribble their ball by using one hand and move from a standing position to a sitting position without stopping their dribble?
9) Now see if you can get back to your feet while dribbling the ball.
10) How many students can balance on one foot only and dribble their ball?
11) Can you dribble the ball 3 times, clap your hands on the 4th count, and then catch the ball?
12) How many different parts of your body can you use to bounce or dribble your ball?

PARTNER CHALLENGES
The next group of tasks will be done using a partner. One ball should be turned in from each partner team. Partners stand 6 to 8 feet apart.
1) Holding the ball with 2 hands over-head, can you pass it to your partner?
2) What other ways can you pass it to your partner by using 2 hands? (Bounce pass, chest pass, underhand, etc.)
3) Can you use just one hand and pass the ball overhead to your partner?
4) What other ways can you pass the ball to your partner by using just *one* hand?
5) Who can use their head to hit the ball to their partner? (Ball should be tossed about 1½ feet above head level with *forehead* striking the ball at the hairline.)
6) As a final challenge, show me how many different ways you can get the ball to your partner.

Lesson 2   STATION ◁1▷ REBOUNDER   25th Week

PERFORMANCE OBJECTIVES
By jumping rope while rebounding on a rebounder, student demonstrates bilateral coordination, body awareness, and dynamic balance.

EQUIPMENT
Rebounder, jump rope, and mats.

CHALLENGES
1) *REVIEW: REBOUNDING WITH ROPE TURNING* – Student rebounds over rebounder center while rhythmically turning a rope at side of body. Both ends of rope are held in one hand.
2) *REBOUNDING WITH ROPE JUMPING* – Student rebounds over rebounder center while jumping a rope. Student must develop coordinated rhythm in jumping the rope. (This is an advanced stunt that some students will not be ready for. They should continue to practice rebounding with rope turning at side of body.)

(2)

STRESS: *REBOUNDING WITH ROPE JUMPING* – Rope must be proper length so it does not catch on edge of rebounder and student is able to maintain correct body alignment (not leaning forward). Elbows stay close to body as rope is turned and jumped.

Lesson 2   STATION ◁2▷ MAT STUNTS   25th Week

PERFORMANCE OBJECTIVES
By *frog head balancing* and performing *push-up to forward roll*, student demonstrates static balance, body and spatial awareness, kinesthesis and gross-motor coordination.

(1)

EQUIPMENT
  Mats.

CHALLENGES
  1) *FROG HEAD BALANCE* - Also called "3 point balance". Student kneels on mat and assumes a tripod position. The hands and forehead form a triangle with the forehead resting slightly forward on the mat. The arms are placed comfortably about a shoulder's width apart on the mat. The knees are lifted forward and placed on top of the bent elbows while the forehead remains placed against the mat. The student balances his or her body in this position with the feet off the mat. (Several students can practice this stunt at the same time working across the mats. Each student can work with a spotter-partner.)
  2) *PUSH-UP TO FORWARD ROLL* - Student assumes *push-up* position on mat with body extended and weight supported on hands and feet. Student walks feet forward toward hands using short steps until feet are fairly close to hands. From this position, student tucks head under and performs a *forward roll* with knees pulled in towards chest as student rolls onto back.

STRESS: *FROG HEAD BALANCE* - Hands are placed flat on mat with fingers spread for better support. The forehead, *not* the top of the head, is placed against the mat to balance on. The tripod (triangle) position is important for proper support. *PUSH-UP TO FORWARD ROLL* - The back of the head, *not* top of the head, touches the mat on roll forward.

Lesson 2   STATION ◇3◇ JUMP BOX   25th Week

PERFORMANCE OBJECTIVES
  By moving up coordination ladder, hopping from jump box, and landing in tire, student demonstrates locomotor coordination, space awareness, laterality, and dynamic balance.

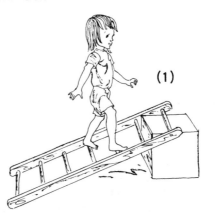
(1)

EQUIPMENT
  Jump box with coordination ladder, red bike tire, cross bar and mats.

CHALLENGES
  1) Student performs *balance walk* on rungs of ladder up to top of box, and then *hops* from box on *right* foot. Student attempts to land in "red" tire on right foot only and hold balance on this foot.
  2) Student performs same task as above using *left* foot for *hopping*.
  3) Student moves up ladder on hands and feet (*dog walk*) and then *jumps* from box and lands in "red" tire. Student performs a *forward roll* out of tire.
  4) For added challenge in above tasks, add cross bar between box and tire.

STRESS: When hopping from box, take-off and landing is made on the same foot. Landing is made in tire on "ball" of foot, not on toes or flat-footed. Hips raised high on *forward roll* by straightening of legs.

Lesson 2   STATION ◇4◇ LOW AND INTERMEDIATE WALKING BOARDS   25th Week

PERFORMANCE OBJECTIVES
  By tossing bean bags and balls to partner on low or intermediate board, student demonstrates dynamic balance, hand-eye coordination, and awareness of position in space.

EQUIPMENT
  Low and intermediate walking boards, ball, bean bag and mats.

(2)

CHALLENGES

1) *BALL TOSS* – The low and intermediate boards are set up about 4 feet apart. One partner starts walking slowly on the low board while the other partner starts on the intermediate board. They both start on the *same end*, and attempt to maintain balance while tossing a rubber ball *back and forth* until reaching the end of their board.

2) *BEAN BAG TOSS* – Partners start on *opposite ends* of boards and move towards each other. One on low board and one on the intermediate board. They attempt to toss and catch the bean bag back and forth as they slowly move towards each other. When they reach the middle of their boards (about side by side), they perform a ½ turn and walk backwards to the end of their boards, but still continue to play catch with the bean bag. (Boards are placed side by side.)

STRESS: Walking the board slowly with eyes focusing on the ball or bean bag. Partners should use an underhand toss when playing catch.

Lesson 3   GAME - *SERVE AND RUN*   25th Week

PERFORMANCE OBJECTIVES

By performing in the *Serve And Run* game, student demonstrates skills in striking a ball, running around an obstacle and fielding a ball.

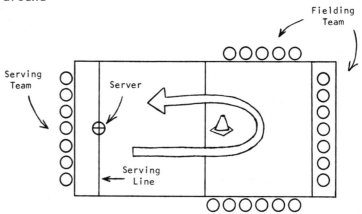

EQUIPMENT

Ball and traffic cone or bowling pin.

DIRECTIONS

1) Two teams are selected with one team designated as the serving team and the other as the fielding team.

2) The serving team lines up side by side behind one end line of the playing court with students waiting their turn to serve (strike) the ball.

3) The fielding team lines up around the opposite *half* of the playing court as shown in the diagram. Students space themselves evenly around the side lines and end line of court.

4) The first server stands behind the serving line as shown and using an underhand striking action, hits the ball using either an open or closed hand. The ball must go forward into the playing court in order to be a fair serve (hit).

5) As soon as the ball is hit, the server attempts to run *around* the traffic cone or pin and get back across the serving line before a student on the fielding team retrieves the ball and runs with it over the serving line.

6) One point is scored if the server makes it back first across the line. If the fielder gets back first with the ball, an out is made.

7) Sides may be changed either on a designated number of outs (3-5) or after each student on the serving team has had his or her turn to sock the ball.

8) Team scoring the most points at conclusion of playing time would be declared the winner.

9) Other rules which should be used are as follows: a) A ball served and hitting *first outside* of the court is a foul ball and must be replayed; b) A ball *leaving* the court before passing over the center court line is a foul ball; c) Two foul balls is an out (optional).

TEACHING SUGGESTIONS

1) Do not allow a few students on the fielding team to "hog" the ball. Only students near where the ball is rolling should be permitted to field it.

2) After students understand the game, they (the fielding team) should be taught how to rotate positions after each new server. Students move one position to their right with the end student nearest the center court line moving across the court.

MULTI-PURPOSE GAME COURT

The Multi-Purpose Game Court illustrated below (not drawn to scale) is designed to be a
court area which can be easily painted on asphalt or other hard-top playground surfaces
and is not only perfect for Level-2 Perceptual-Motor/Movement Exploration related games,
but is easily adaptable to a wide variety of game and relay activities. This game court
is especially valuable for use on small size playgrounds with limited hardtop area. It
includes lines for end zones as used in team games, as well as different size circles and
dotted relay lines. Almost any type of game can be adapted to this court, thus making it
a "must" on every school playground. Teachers find that readily available court markings
allow for ease and efficiency in organizing and conducting game experiences.

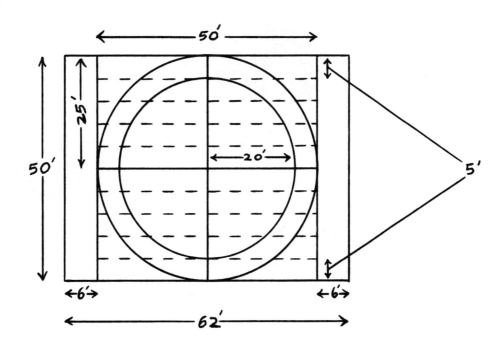

OVERVIEW OF BASIC PERCEPTUAL-MOTOR EQUIPMENT

SCOOTER BOARD

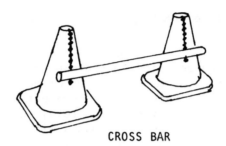

CROSS BAR

AUTO TIRE
IN SUPPORT STAND

REBOUNDER

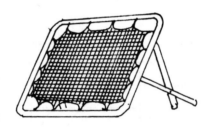

REBOUND NET

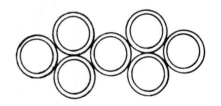

LAUNCHING BOARD

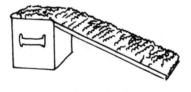

BICYCLE TIRE PATTERN

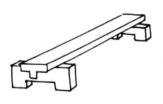

WALKING BOARD

JUMP BOX

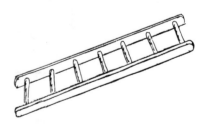

COORDINATION LADDER

EQUIPMENT CONSTRUCTION DIAGRAMS

On the following pages, only the equipment that can be easily constructed is diagramed. Other equipment such as the bouncer, rebound net, etc., is more involved in its construction and design and should be ordered from suppliers.

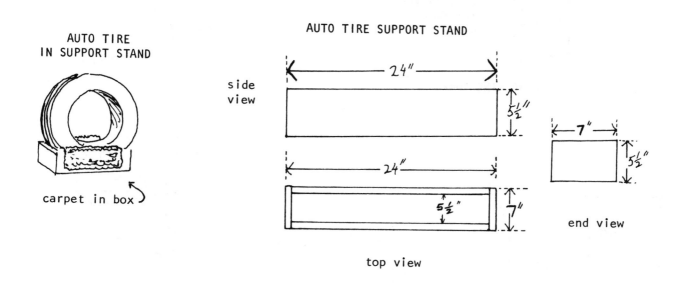

AUTO TIRE IN SUPPORT STAND

carpet in box

AUTO TIRE SUPPORT STAND

side view — 24" — 5½"

top view — 24" — 5½" — 7"

end view — 7" — 5½"

JUMP BOX

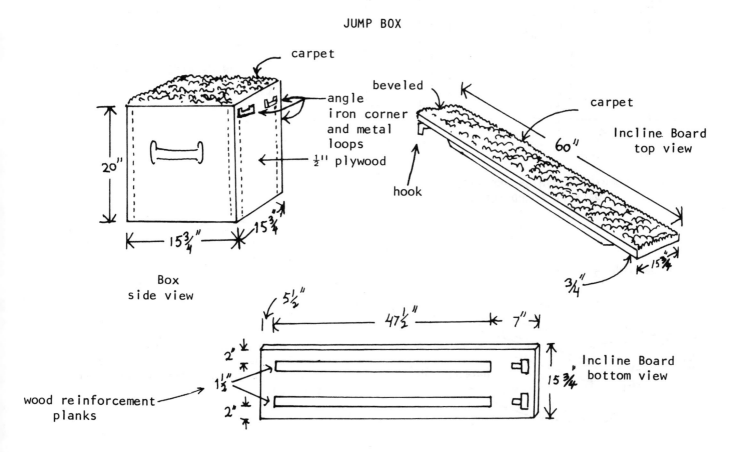

carpet

angle iron corner and metal loops

½" plywood

20"

15¾" 15¾"

Box side view

beveled

carpet

hook

Incline Board top view

60"

15¾"

¾"

wood reinforcement planks

5½"

47½" 7"

2" 1½" 2"

15¾"

Incline Board bottom view

WALKING BOARD

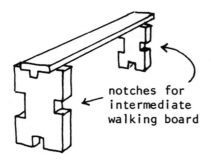

notches for
intermediate
walking board

HIGH WALKING BOARD

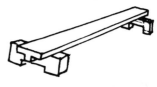

LOW WALKING BOARD

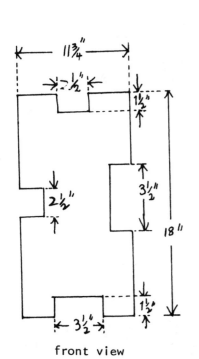

front view

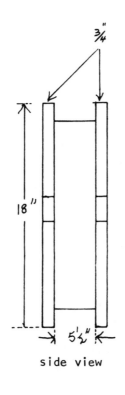

side view

COMBINATION HIGH AND INTERMEDIATE
WALKING BOARD SUPPORTS

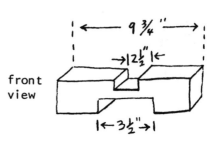

front view

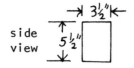

side view

LOW WALKING BOARD SUPPORT

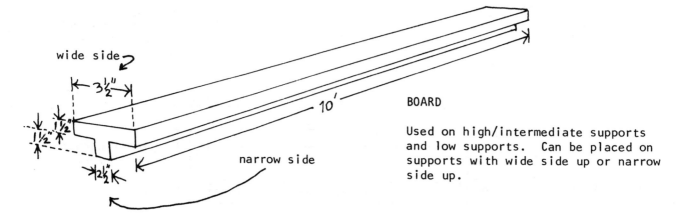

wide side

narrow side

BOARD

Used on high/intermediate supports
and low supports. Can be placed on
supports with wide side up or narrow
side up.

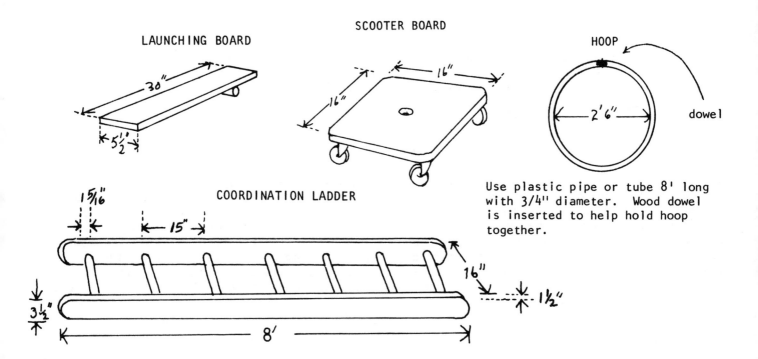

LAUNCHING BOARD

SCOOTER BOARD

HOOP

dowel

Use plastic pipe or tube 8' long with 3/4" diameter. Wood dowel is inserted to help hold hoop together.

COORDINATION LADDER

CROSS BARS & TRAFFIC CONES

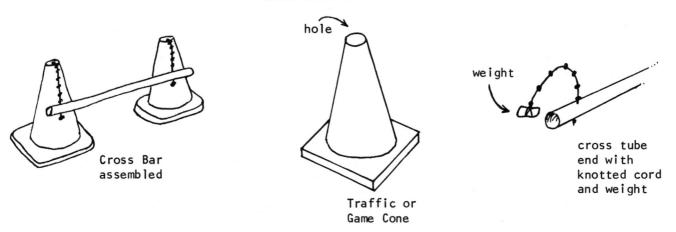

hole

weight

Cross Bar assembled

Traffic or Game Cone

cross tube end with knotted cord and weight

CROSS BARS

This type of cross bar can be easily assembled by combining two traffic or game cones and a plastic cross tube (plastic tubes that golf clubs fit into, or thin walled plastic pipe). The plastic cross tubes are 3 feet in length. The cross tube is held to the cones by small knotted ropes or cords. The cords are attached to the tube and hang down loose inside of the cones. Weights, which are attached to the ends of the cords inside of the cones, hold the cross tube in place. The height of the cross tube is easily adjusted since the attached weighted ropes are knotted (to catch on the cone edge) and hang free inside of the cones.

NOTE: Cross bars are interchangeable with jump standards and both serve the same purpose of providing an obstacle to go over or under.

TRAFFIC CONES (GAME CONES)

Cones are not only used in constructing cross bars, but also serve as useful obstacles by themselves. Plastic or rubber cones which have holes in their tops and are about 18 inches high make the best components of cross bars.

ROPES

Get 100 to 200 foot coils of 3/8 inch cotton sash cord or rope. (Polyethelene cords are also suitable.) Cut the cord into 7 or 8 foot lengths. Tape, knot, or melt (in the case of polyethelene cords) the ends to prevent unraveling.

BEAN BAGS

Bean bags can be easily made. Just use a durable fabric like sailcloth, denim, burlap, etc. Cut material into 8" X 4" rectangles. Fold 8" side in half. On the sewing machine, using a short stitch length and sewing 1/4" from the outer edges, sew along 2 sides. Leave the 3rd side open so bag can be turned inside out to hide the stitching and be filled. After turning the bag inside out, use a pinking shear, and pink along the open edges of the bag. Fill bag 3/4 full with either rice, small beans, or aquarium gravel. Use 2 extra long paper clips or bobby pins to hold filling in while sewing a row of stitches 1/2" from pinked edge. If you like, for reinforcement, sew a 2nd row of stitches 3/8" from pinked edge.

RHYTHM STICKS

Can be made from dowels, broom handles, plastic tubing, plastic pipes, etc. For best results, sticks should be at least 12" long and have a diameter from 5/8" to one inch. An easy inexpensive (if not free) way to make Rhythm Sticks is by making the sticks out of old newspapers. Students can easily accomplish this in a class project. Simply take the complete section of a newspaper, such as the Sports Section, leave the paper folded, and tightly roll the paper from the narrow width side of the paper to the opposite narrow side. Roll of paper is then held together by winding masking tape around it.

SOME THOUGHTS ON EQUIPMENT CONSTRUCTION

Most of the perceptual-motor equipment in this curriculum guide is relatively simple to construct. Equipment construction would make an excellent project for junior-high and senior-high school wood and metal shops. It would not only be inexpensive, but would provide a valuable learning experience. Equipment could be literally "made to order" for your particular perceptual-motor needs.

Another possibility is a local carpenter or lumber yard and/or local metal shop. This would give business to your local area, help in generating community support, and, in many cases, be less expensive. As in the case of school district wood and metal shop classes, you would be able to work closely with them and get a "tailor made" product. Many large equipment manufacturers started out in someone's garage making products for local schools and institutions.

Some other ideas that come to mind are organizations such as the Goodwill, and handicapped centers, etc. They are ready, willing, and able to make good quality equipment items to your specifications at somewhat above cost. When you give them your business, you not only get quality equipment made to the exact specifications for your situation, but you are also helping them.

PROGRAM SUPPLIERS

The publisher, Front Row Experience, and many educational stores in the United States, Canada, and Australia sell the printed components of Jack Capon's Perceptual-Motor Program, Levels 1 and 2. The equipment components of Jack's Program can be found in most sports equipment stores and some educational stores. Although most equipment items will be found to vary from the exact specifications called for, they will be near enough so that they can be easily adapted to the Program. The publisher also sells some equipment items. For a free brochure on all products sold by the publisher, write directly to: Front Row Experience, 540 Discovery Bay Blvd., Byron, California 94514.

PROGRAM EQUIPMENT LIST

The following equipment list shows the types of equipment needed and how many of each. Most of the equipment listed here was illustrated in the Overview Of Basic Perceptual-Motor Equipment and in the Equipment Construction Diagrams beginning on pages 86 and 87 respectively.

The individual cost of equipment items is not given because of constant price fluctuations. However, of the total equipment cost, you'll find nearly half of it is borne by "tumbling mats". If your school already has mats, then you will save quite a bit. Any other similar equipment items you already have will save you still more. Your school or district may be able to make some equipment inexpensively. Also, some items such as bicycle and car tires can many times be obtained free (in worn or damaged condition, but useable) from bike and car repair shops, etc.

Equipment Needed	Quantity	Equipment Needed	Quantity
Low Walking Board (7" off ground)	1	Combination Intermediate/High Walking Board (11" to 20½" off ground)	1
Coordination Ladder (8' long)	1	Jump Box with Incline Board (20" high x 15' 3/4" wide)	1
Launching Board	1		
Rebounder (jogging exerciser) 40" dia frame, 8" high	1	Plastic Cross Tubes with weighted cord	3 } makes 3 cross bars
Scooter Board (large 16" x 16")	1	Game Cones (18" high)	6
Rebound Net (36" x 36")	1	Tire Holder (24" long x 7" wide)	1
Tumbling Mats (4' x 6')	6	Rubber Balls (6" to 8" diameter)	4
Plastic Hoops (30" diameter)	12	Parachute (24' to 30' in diameter)	1
Ropes (7' long, 3/8" diameter)	6	Bicycle Tires (used, large size)	12
Auto Tire (used, **large size**)	1	Rhythm Sticks (set of 24 four color sticks with activity booklet)	2 sets
Tracking Ball (small plastic ball on cord)	1	Bean Bags (set of 12 denim bags with activity booklet)	2 sets

ADDING MORE PERCEPTUAL-MOTOR LEARNING STATIONS

The use of learning stations in your Perceptual-Motor Program enables you to provide a challenging environment for movement in which a task centered approach can be used to make the Program fun and exciting for all students. A variety of equipment is important so that the learning environment can be frequently changed or manipulated, and lessons can be sequenced for proper skill development.

POINTS FOR CONSIDERATION

1) Organize at least 3 to 5 stations depending on the number of participants so that groups will be small for more active participation.
2) Use movement tasks that allow for successful participation by all students. (Group by skill level, if necessary.)
3) Focus on challenges (tasks) that stress control and accuracy of movement.
4) Rotate groups often to keep interest at a high level.
5) Be constantly aware of safety factors. Like: a) adequate space for movement; b) mats under certain equipment items; c) speed of movement; d) type of clothing worn; etc.

TYPES OF STATIONS

1) *Walking Boards* (balance beams) at various heights used along with obstacles for balance and laterality training.
2) *Mats* for a variety of mat stunts such as crawling, animal movements, rolls, etc.
3) *Box or Bench* combined with tires for jumping off of and onto mat to develop locomotor control and balance.
4) *Bicycle Tires* in a pattern for jumping, hopping, and ball skill challenges.
5) *Game Cones* with cross tube and tires in a pattern for jumping and hopping challenges
6) *Hoops* in a pattern for jumping, hopping, and ball skill challenges.
7) *Ropes* in a criss-cross pattern for jumping and hopping challenges.
8) *Boxes or Barrels* for crawling through.
9) *Bowling Pins or Game Cones* for use as target in rolling balls or for obstacles to dribble ball around.
10) *Bouncer* (modified trampoline or inner tube with canvas cover) for bouncing activities to improve balance and body awareness.
11) *Coordination Ladder* (wood with rungs) for various types of movement tasks such as walking on the rungs, jumping between the rungs, animal walks on the ladder, etc.
12) *Climbing Ladder* ("A" frame type) for basic climbing experiences to develop coordination of arms and legs, and overcome fear of height.
13) *Rebound Net* for throwing and catching skills (hand-eye coordination activities).
14) *Launching Board* which combines foot-eye and hand-eye coordination experiences. Student steps on board and launches up bean bags or balls.
15) *Springboard* for jumping and body control experiences. Students spring from board and land in bicycle tires, etc.
16) *Tire Holder with Auto Tire* (carpeted box or metal stand to hold tire upright) for crawling through without touching the tire.
17) *Scooter Board* for coordination challenges either in a prone, kneeling, or sitting position on the board.
18) *Geometric Shapes* in supports for form discrimination challenges involving crawling through the shapes.
19) *Portable Jump Standard* with cross bar for crawling under, jumping over, etc.
20) *Bean Bags* with tires or shapes as targets for hand-eye coordination tasks.
21) *Waste Paper Baskets* as targets for basket shooting or bean bag tossing.
22) *Balance Board* (square board on center piece) for balance and laterality training.

FREE CATALOG !

**Write for our Free catalog of Innovative Curriculum Guidebooks And Materials
for MOVEMENT EDUCATION, SPECIAL EDUCATION and PERCEPTUAL-MOTOR DEVELOPMENT**

FRONT ROW EXPERIENCE
540 Discovery Bay Blvd.
Byron, CA 94515-9454

Call Toll-Free: 1-800-524-9091